The Professional Scrum Master (PSM I) Guide

Successfully practice Scrum with real-world projects and achieve your PSM I certification with confidence

Fred Heath

BIRMINGHAM—MUMBAI

The Professional Scrum Master (PSM I) Guide

Group Product Manager: Kunal Chaudhari
Publishing Product Manager: Shweta Bairoliya
Senior Editor: Storm Mann
Content Development Editor: Nithya Sadanandan
Technical Editor: Gaurav Gala
Copy Editor: Safis Editing
Project Coordinator: Deeksha Thakkar
Proofreader: Safis Editing
Indexer: Vinayak Purushotham
Production Designer: Ponraj Dhandapani

First published: June 2021

Production reference: 2130122

Published by Packt Publishing Ltd.
Livery Place
35 Livery Street
Birmingham
B3 2PB, UK.

ISBN 978-1-80020-556-7

www.packt.com

To my wife, Julie, and my daughter, Sophia. They make it all worthwhile.

- Fred Heath

Contributors

About the author

Fred Heath is a senior software engineer with 24 years' experience. Fred has worked at every level of the software development lifecycle and has used a multitude of technologies, platforms, and programming languages. His professional interests include programming in Ruby and Elixir, behavior-driven development, and semantic analysis.

Fred holds B.Eng and M.Sc. degrees (Cardiff University) and is a Microsoft Certified Professional (SQL Server 2000), a certified Professional Scrum Master (PSM-I), and a certified Professional Agile Leader (PAL-I). He enjoys blogging about software development topics and is a frequent speaker at conferences and meetups.

Fred has also authored *Managing Software Requirements the Agile Way* (Packt, 2020).

About the reviewer

Tarun Gupta is a certified Scrum Master with around 14 years of experience in IT. He has several credentials, including PMI-ACP, PSM II, CSM, ASM, SAFe Agilist 4.5, and PMP.

He started his career as a QA engineer in the telecom domain after graduating with a master's degree in computer applications (MCA) from Pune University in 2007. He has helped teams to transition from Waterfall to Agile and has coached them to achieve maximum efficiency and the highest product value by successfully completing sprints.

Tarun believes that Scrum has some important values, such as focus, commitment, openness, respect, and courage, that can be adopted in life to be more productive and successful. He believes that any organization can be Agile if there is transparency, continuous improvement, continuous delivery, and adaptability.

Table of Contents

3
The Scrum Team

4
Scrum Events

5
Scrum Artifacts

Section 2: Scrum in Action

6

Planning and Estimating with Scrum

7

The Sprint Journey

8

Facets of Scrum

Section 3: The PSM Certification

9

Preparing for the PSM I Assessment

Assessments

Other Books You May Enjoy

Index

Preface

The Scrum framework was conceived in the late 1980s to counteract the formal, rigid, and stagnating software development methodologies prevalent at the time. The Scrum framework was formalized in the mid-1990s and its founders, Jeff Sutherland and Ken Schwaber, were instrumental in the creation of the Agile Manifesto and the subsequent spread of the Agile development movement. Scrum quickly became the most popular Agile framework, with huge adoption in both small businesses and the enterprise world. Part of the popularity of Scrum is its adaptability. The Scrum Guide keeps getting updated every few years to reflect current thinking and practices. Scrum.org also offers an impressive array of Scrum-related resources and certifications, one of which we'll be addressing in this book.

This book aims to teach people new to, or inexperienced with, Scrum all about the Scrum framework from a practical as well as a theoretical perspective. The book consists of two parts. In the first five chapters, we will cover the Scrum fundamentals. The theory and principles of Scrum will be digested, before moving on to cover the Scrum Team, Events, and Artifacts. The second part will focus on more practical knowledge, by examining practices and methods used by Scrum Teams in the real world. We will learn how to plan and estimate in Scrum, how to monitor progress and deal with different situations within the Sprint, best practices for infrastructure and testing, and how to manage eventualities such as technical debt or remote working. Every chapter closes with a short quiz to reinforce the knowledge gained.

Finally, the last chapter is entirely dedicated to the PSM I assessment. It offers practical advice on what to do before, during, and after the assessment exam to maximize your chances of success. This is capped with a mock assessment questionnaire, which closely represents the actual PSM I assessment.

Who this book is for

This book is for professionals who want to build a strong foundation in Scrum practices and development. Project managers, product owners, product managers across various industries, sectors, and departments, software architects, developers, coders, and testers looking to achieve PSM certification will also find this book helpful.

It may also serve as a useful source of updated knowledge for existing Scrum Masters or developers who are not fully cognizant of the 2020 Scrum Guide revisions. Having existing Scrum, or other Agile methodology, knowledge is not a prerequisite for reading this book.

What this book covers

Chapter 1, Introduction to Scrum, presents you with the history and motivation behind Scrum, its value as a development framework, and introduces you to the PSM I assessment.

Chapter 2, Scrum Theory and Principles, shares knowledge of the fundamental concepts behind Scrum, its values, and its pillars. It also highlights the value and effect of these concepts in applying Scrum successfully.

Chapter 3, The Scrum Team, analyzes the role and responsibilities of the Scrum Master, Product Owner, and Developers and their interactions within the Scrum development lifecycle.

Chapter 4, Scrum Events, explains the significance of the Sprint, Sprint Planning, Daily Scrum, Sprint Review, and Sprint Retrospective events and their application and utility within the Scrum development lifecycle.

Chapter 5, Scrum Artifacts, details the Product Backlog, the Sprint Backlog, and the Product Increment, as well as the commitments undertaken for each of these Artifacts. The inter-dependencies of these Artifacts are also covered.

Chapter 6, Planning and Estimating with Scrum, delves into the world of measuring, estimating, planning, and forecasting. You will learn how to calculate your team's velocity, create a product roadmap, and measure your progress with burn-up and burn-down charts.

Chapter 7, The Sprint Journey, imparts practical advice and techniques for day-to-day working during the Sprint. Product Backlog refinement is explained, as well as how to use a Scrum Board in different scenarios, manage defects, and what to do if the Sprint is canceled.

Chapter 8, Facets of Scrum, covers best practices to use when working with Scrum. The importance of a CI/CD pipeline as testing levels is examined in detail. Techniques for managing technical debt, working remotely, and scaling Scrum are also explained.

Chapter 9, Preparing for the PSM I Assessment, is a short chapter mainly hosting 25 quiz questions summarizing the knowledge contained in this book, helping you to prepare for taking the PSM I assessment exam. Practical advice on how to prepare for the exam, and what to do during and after, is also given.

Download the color images

We also provide a PDF file that has color images of the screenshots/diagrams used in this book. You can download it here:

```
https://static.packt-cdn.com/downloads/9781800205567_
ColorImages.pdf
```

Conventions used

There are a number of text conventions used throughout this book.

Bold: Indicates a new term, an important word, or words that you see onscreen. For example, words in menus or dialog boxes appear in the text like this. Here is an example: "Integrate the gadget database in the **Show Gadgets** page."

> **Tips or important notes**
> Appear like this.

Get in touch

Feedback from our readers is always welcome.

General feedback: If you have questions about any aspect of this book, mention the book title in the subject of your message and email us at customercare@packtpub.com.

Errata: Although we have taken every care to ensure the accuracy of our content, mistakes do happen. If you have found a mistake in this book, we would be grateful if you would report this to us. Please visit www.packtpub.com/support/errata, selecting your book, clicking on the Errata Submission Form link, and entering the details.

Piracy: If you come across any illegal copies of our works in any form on the Internet, we would be grateful if you would provide us with the location address or website name. Please contact us at copyright@packt.com with a link to the material.

If you are interested in becoming an author: If there is a topic that you have expertise in and you are interested in either writing or contributing to a book, please visit authors.packtpub.com.

Share Your Thoughts

Once you've read *The Professional Scrum Master (PSM I) Guide*, we'd love to hear your thoughts! Scan the QR code below to go straight to the Amazon review page for this book and share your feedback.

https://packt.link/r/1800205562

Your review is important to us and the tech community and will help us make sure we're delivering excellent quality content.

Section 1: The Scrum Framework

In this part, you will learn why and when to use Scrum and explore the components of the Scrum framework.

This section comprises the following chapters:

- *Chapter 1, Introduction to Scrum*
- *Chapter 2, Scrum Theory and Principles*
- *Chapter 3, The Scrum Team*
- *Chapter 4, Scrum Events*
- *Chapter 5, Scrum Artifacts*

1
Introduction to Scrum

In this chapter, we will introduce Scrum as an Agile framework, defining both Agile and Scrum and discussing the history and principles behind them. We will then explain the value of using the iterative and incremental development lifecycle prescribed by Scrum and describe some of the other Scrum benefits. We will close this chapter by introducing the PSM assessments and talking about the PSM I assessment in more detail. We will cover the following topics:

- What is Agile software development?

- What is Scrum?

- The value of an iterative and incremental approach

- Why should you choose Scrum?

- Introducing PSM I assessment

By the end of this chapter, you should know what Agile development and the Scrum framework are, how they improve and optimize software development, and what the PSM assessment involves. Let's start by understanding what people mean by the term **Agile**.

What is Agile software development?

Anyone who has been working in software development over the last 10 years or so will have at least heard of the term **Agile**. People often talk about *doing Agile* or *being Agile* but, beyond a cool-sounding buzzword, what is Agile really all about? Well, to answer that question, we need to look at the origins of Agile software development.

Back in the late 1990s, many senior software developers and industry leaders, fed up with the static and inflexible software development methodologies prevalent at the time, were already experimenting with more flexible and responsive techniques and approaches. In 2000 and 2001, a small group of these influencers met up to discuss these methods and techniques. The unifying theme behind this effort was a desire to be able to quickly deliver working software to end users and to get rapid feedback on the software's impact and scope. In the forthcoming years, methodologies developed under this philosophy came to be known under the umbrella term of *Agile*.

The Agile philosophy is best captured in the *Agile Manifesto* (2001), which identifies the following values:

- Individuals and interactions over processes and tools
- Working software over comprehensive documentation
- Customer collaboration over contract negotiation
- Responding to change over following a plan

The Agile Manifesto clearly states that *while there is value in the items on the right of this list, we value the items on the left more.* So, it is not an abandonment of the old values, but a realization that some new values (individuals and interactions, working software, collaboration, adapting to change) are far more relevant in the modern software development world. In addition, they also came up with a set of principles (see *Principles behind the Agile Manifesto* in the *Further reading* section), emphasizing continuous delivery, frequent feedback, personal interactions, and much more. These principles are as follows:

- Our highest priority is to satisfy the customer through early and continuous delivery of valuable software.
- Welcome changing requirements, even late in development. Agile processes harness change for the customer's competitive advantage.

- Deliver working software frequently, from every couple of weeks to every couple of months, with a preference for a shorter timescale.

- Businesspeople and developers must work together daily throughout the project.

- Build projects around motivated individuals.

- Give them the environment and support they need and trust them to get the job done.

- The most efficient and effective method of conveying information to and within a development team is face-to-face conversation.

- Working software is the primary measure of progress.

- Agile processes promote sustainable development.

- The sponsors, developers, and users should be able to maintain a constant pace indefinitely.

- Continuous attention to technical excellence and good design enhances agility.

- Simplicity – the art of maximizing the amount of work not done – is essential.

- The best architectures, requirements, and designs emerge from self-organizing teams.

- At regular intervals, the team reflects on how to become more effective, then tunes and adjusts its behavior accordingly.

It becomes clear that *Agile* is not a specific methodology, process, or framework but more of a mindset; a set of principles and ideals to guide us through the software development process.

This is a rather important concept to keep in mind: throughout my career, I've heard managers, directors, and developers boasting about *being Agile* because they have daily stand-up meetings, practice pair-programming, or use a Kanban board (more on these in *Chapter 7, The Sprint Journey*). All these are perfectly good tools to support an Agile development lifecycle, but their use alone does not make us Agile any more than wearing a cape and my underwear outside my pants makes me a superhero. To truly be Agile, you have to think and act in an Agile manner, that is in a manner consistent with the Agile Manifesto. One of the most popular ways of being Agile is by applying Scrum in your organization or team.

With this in mind, let's take a closer look at the Scrum framework.

What is Scrum?

In the previous section, we mentioned that in the late 1990s several visionaries were experimenting with flexible and adaptive ways to develop software. Two of these visionaries were Ken Schwaber and Jeff Sutherland. They came up with an Agile framework called **Scrum**, which was based on using the scientific method of empiricism, rather than strictly following a pre-defined plan. Scrum embraces Agile, not only because it was created by two of the people involved in the creation of the Agile Manifesto, but also because the Scrum values are actively derived from Agile principles (see *Scrum Values meet Agile Principles* in the *Further reading* section). In fact, most organizations that have adopted Agile methods use Scrum (see *The State of Agile* in the *Further reading* section).

It is important to emphasize that Scrum is a *process framework*, not a process by itself. It introduces a number of rules, milestones, and checkpoints that must be adhered to, regardless of the underlying development process. The Scrum framework can be used to contain a varied number of popular development methodologies, processes, or techniques, as per the organization's working practices. Scrum doesn't tell us how to perform our work, it just sets up a container within which to perform it. We can use whichever development methods and design or release processes we like, within Scrum. As long as these abide by the Agile and Scrum principles, it is absolutely fine to do so.

Scrum encourages the adoption of values such as respect for people, openness, and commitment in order to help us to cope with uncertainty and solving complex problems. It promotes the creation of self-organizing and cross-functional teams that are able to deliver working software independently and in spite of ever-changing external requirements and circumstances.

The Scrum framework consists of three components:

- **The Scrum Team**: A self-organizing, cross-functional set of people who will deliver the working software.

- **Scrum Events**: A number of time-boxed events that help create regularity, provide feedback, foster self-adjustment, and promote an iterative and incremental lifecycle.

- **Scrum Artifacts**: Items that represent work or added value and that provide transparency for the team's work progress and achievements. Artifacts are also the cornerstone of inspection and adaptation.

The Scrum Team attends Scrum Events and creates Scrum Artifacts as well as working software. Events are attended at predetermined intervals and may trigger the generation or modification of artifacts. Artifacts may be inspected by the team but also by external inspectors. The following diagram illustrates these interactions:

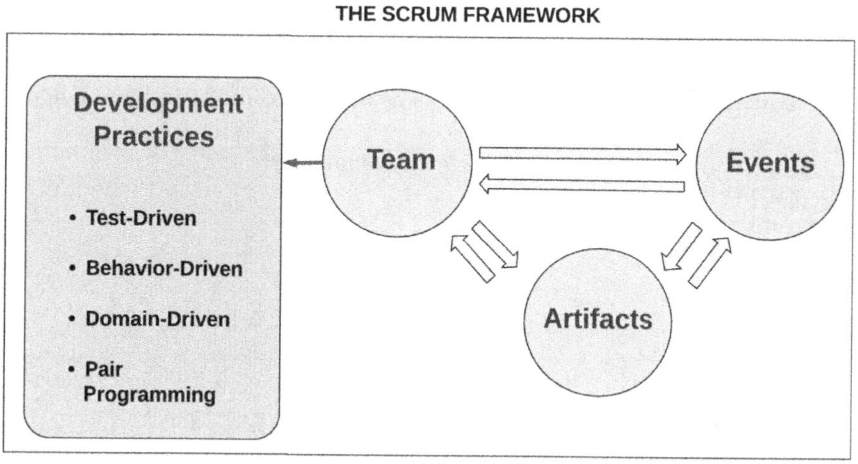

THE SCRUM FRAMEWORK

Figure 1.1 – The Scrum framework components

The usefulness of Scrum lies in its three main components (**Teams**, **Events**, and **Artifacts**) and their interactions. We'll be discussing these components and interactions in detail in *Chapters 3, The Scrum Team, Chapter 4, Scrum Events*, and *Chapter 5, Scrum Artifacts*.

For now, let's take a look at one of the ways Scrum makes us work more efficiently and productively with the adoption of an iterative and incremental development lifecycle.

The value of an iterative and incremental approach

One of the greatest benefits of using Scrum is that it prescribes an iterative and incremental approach to software development. This is by far the most effective and efficient approach for creating software in today's world and in the next sections, we'll explain exactly why that is the case. Let's begin by remembering how we used to develop software...

The waterfall legacy

When I first started programming, we used to build our systems in distinct, single stages: first analysis, then design, then coding, and so on. Each stage would cover everything we would need to consider in order to deliver the whole system, down to the finest detail. Once the stage was complete, we would move on to the next stage of the development lifecycle and never re-visit the previous, completed stage. This is now known as the **waterfall approach** because each stage was like a distinct level of a waterfall, one following the other in sequential, non-repeatable fashion, as illustrated in the following figure:

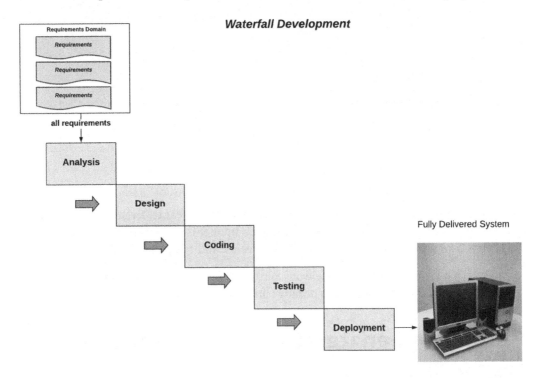

Figure 1.2 – Waterfall development

As we soon came to discover, there were some serious drawbacks to this approach:

- First, it took a long time to actually deliver software to our users. Since we had to consider every possible requirement, and design and document every possible functionality before we could start coding, it would take months or often years to progress from system inception to system deployment. By that time, a competitor would have beaten us to the punch by delivering their system first or the business need for our system would have simply passed, overtaken by circumstances and changes in the market.

- Secondly, since we were moving sequentially from stage to stage, any design flaws or false assumptions that were discovered after deployment could not be fixed without a major re-haul of our system. This took a lot of time and effort.

- Finally, if requirements were changed by the customer once we were past the design stage, we would have to start pretty much from scratch again.

In short, the waterfall approach was inflexible, risky, and time-consuming. It worked well for projects with rigid, unchanging requirements that were not affected by market conditions and weren't time-critical. However, as software applications started to become more prevalent in our lives and the market expanded and diversified, such projects started becoming rarer. Gone were the days in which consumers were happy to sit and wait for the next version of their spreadsheet application to come out from one of the two companies that produced them, or to wait for their email provider to fix a bug in their email system due to there being no real alternative.

Today, customers have plenty of choices and they value the speedy delivery of working software over dependence on monopolistic software providers. For software providers nowadays, time-to-market is an essential factor in their strategy and waterfall development is just too risky and rigid to follow. Luckily, the people who came up with Agile methodologies saw this at an early stage and almost all of the Agile methodologies that were developed, especially Scrum, follow what is known as an **iterative and incremental development approach**. Let's find out what that means.

Iterative and incremental software development

Iterative development means developing software in small chunks repeatedly, instead of waiting for everything to be finished and delivering a large chunk at the end. It entails breaking down the requirements that need to be implemented and implementing a few at a time. So instead of having a large, big-bang software delivery at the end of the project, we have many smaller deliveries at regular intervals. These delivery intervals are known as **Iterations**. In Scrum, we call an iteration a **sprint**.

Incremental development means that each iteration builds upon software delivered by previous iterations. So, if we implement *Feature A* in our first iteration (let's call this version 1 of our system), then in version 2 our users will expect to see *Feature A* and *another* feature too. Sometimes, we may have to deliver *Feature A* again, but this time working better or faster or having fixed a bug in it. The point is, each iteration should offer something more than the previous one. This chunk of software and functionality that each iteration adds to the system is called an **Increment**. In Scrum, an increment is not randomly produced but is intended to achieve a specific goal, to deliver the desired functionality or to fix a specific problem. This goal is decided at the beginning of the Sprint and is known as a **sprint goal**.

The following figure shows the characteristics of an iterative and incremental development approach:

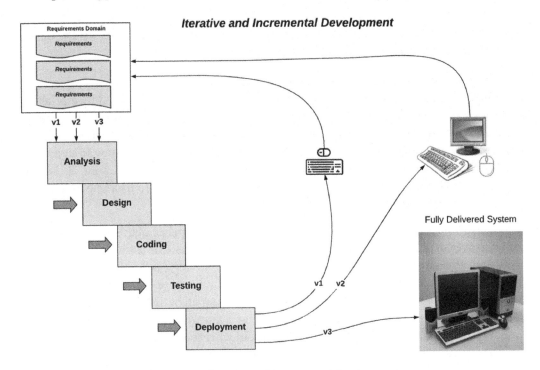

Figure 1.3 – Iterative and incremental development

As shown, in an incremental and iterative development cycle, there is no separation between the development stages. So, within the same iteration, our team may be designing some feature, while coding some other feature, while testing a third one, all at the same time. This approach to development gives the developers the chance to correct any mistakes, fix any issues, and inspect and adapt to changing requirements at an early stage, which means less time and effort and less risk of failure or late delivery.

In an incremental and iterative cycle, we deliver working software at the end of each sprint. So, as illustrated, for **Sprint 1** we deliver a crude version of our product that doesn't do much but outline what we try to build, with some basic functionality. At the end of the sprint, we showcase our software to the stakeholders and receive feedback. At the same time, we come together as the Scrum Team to inspect and review what we did well in the sprint and what we could improve. This gives us valuable information on how to improve the product in the next sprint, but also on how to improve our working practices.

In **Sprint 2**, we apply the lessons learned from **Sprint 1** and deliver a much more functional version of the product with more and better features. Once again, at the end of the sprint, we receive feedback, inspect, and adapt in order to improve both our product and our workflow.

In the final sprint, we deliver the whole product, fully functional. By incorporating the feedback we received and the lessons we learned in the previous sprints, we understand the customer requirements much better and have improved our productivity and teamwork. In fact, inspection and adaptation are key pillars of Scrum (more about these in *Chapter 2*, *Scrum Theory and Principles*), so it's no surprise that the Scrum framework imposes iterative and incremental development. It's one of the many reasons why doing Scrum is so beneficial. But let's look at some other reasons for doing Scrum...

Why should you choose Scrum?

Although Scrum is by far the most popular Agile development framework, it is by no means the only one. **Kanban**, **Lean**, **Extreme Programming (XP)**, **Dynamic System Development Method (DSDM)**, and **Crystal** are all examples of Agile processes, frameworks, or methodologies. I am not going to patronize you by telling you that Scrum is the best approach and you should follow it unquestionably at all times. As with every other tools, you need to decide if its use fits your needs. I advocate Scrum and I use it most of the time, but I once worked on a project where Kanban provided the most fitting approach, due to that project's special circumstances. Some of my fellow Scrum Masters and PSM members have occasionally found that using Lean tool-sets, such as 5S, or applying XP techniques, may suit a specific project's needs better. In fact, many organizations use elements from other Agile approaches in addition to Scrum. However, Scrum is the most popular for good reasons:

- Short, focused iterations allow for quick software delivery to customers
- Constant opportunities for introspection and adaptation allow better product quality and team efficiency
- Scrum's transparency allows external stakeholders to follow progress even without knowing or understanding Scrum

If this is not enough, consider the fact that the overwhelming majority of Scrum users emphatically state that they will continue to use it, that it offers value to their organization, and that it improves work quality (`https://www.scrumalliance.org/learn-about-scrum/state-of-scrum`).

Introducing PSM assessments

Professional Scrum Master (**PSM**) assessments are available to anyone who wishes to validate their depth of knowledge of the Scrum framework and its application. Those who pass the assessment will receive the industry-recognized PSM certification to demonstrate their level of Scrum mastery. To better understand how these assessments came about, let's take a look at how Scrum was organized and evolved.

Scrum organizations and their history

Back in the *What is Scrum?* section, we mentioned how Ken Schwaber and Jeff Sutherland created Scrum back in the 1990s. To better support Scrum and encourage its adoption, Schwaber, Sutherland, and others created the Scrum Alliance in 2002 (`https://www.scrumalliance.org/`). In 2009, Schwaber decided to go his own way and created Scrum.org. These two still remain the only valid and authentic Scrum organizations. They both offer Scrum-related certifications. Scrum.org offers **PSM** certification at two levels: I and II for a fundamental and advanced understanding of Scrum, respectively.

To ensure that both Scrum Alliance and Scrum.org are aligned, that the Scrum content doesn't digress, and that Scrum remains independent of any organization, Schwaber and Sutherland created a public document called *The Scrum Guide* (*Further reading*). The Scrum Guide contains the definition of Scrum and its components and all the rules and responsibilities prescribed by the Scrum framework.

They occasionally revise this document, with the current version being November 2017. This book is based on and uses this version of the Scrum Guide. The Scrum Guide is essential reading for anyone wanting to take the PSM assessments, or indeed anyone practicing Scrum.

Now that we know how the PSM assessments came to be, let's get better acquainted with the PSM I assessment, which is what we'll be focusing on in this book.

The PSM I assessment

Unlike its Scrum Alliance counterpart, the PSM assessment requires passing an online exam. Here are some details on this:

- The exam consists of 80 multiple-choice questions and must be completed within 60 minutes.
- The pass mark is 85%.
- The exam is only offered in the English language.

- Some questions have only one correct answer. Some questions have multiple correct answers. Some questions have only a True/False answer. It is clearly indicated during the exam how many answers are correct for each question

- Not every question has the same weight, so don't think that you need to answer 68 (that is, 85%) questions correctly in order to pass the exam; it could be fewer or more, we just don't know how the questions are weighed.

- The exam costs 150 US dollars, which are payable online by credit card.

There are no official pre-requisites for taking the exam. In other words, Scrum.org does not require you to attend any of their courses, read any of their books, or even have real-life Scrum experience before sitting it. Having said that, allow me to offer you some tips:

- As with any knowledge domain, real-life experience makes a difference when taking an assessment. I know PSM I holders who passed the exam without having worked with Scrum before. However, any experience you have working in an actual Scrum-based organization will increase your odds of passing.

- Books by the Scrum creators, such as *Software in 30 Days: How Agile Managers Beat the Odds, Delight Their Customers, and Leave Competitors in the Dust* in the *Further reading* section, provide some valuable insights that can often prove useful during the exam.

- The Scrum Open Assessment (`https://www.scrum.org/open-assessments/scrum-open`) is an extremely valuable tool to prepare you for the exam. Some of the questions in it often appear during the actual exam. I strongly recommend taking the Open Assessment before taking the actual exam.

We will be covering the PSM I assessment in great detail in *Chapter 9*, *Preparing for the PSM I Assessment*.

Summary

In this chapter, we discussed the concept of Agile development and its nature as a specific philosophy, guided by certain values and principles. Adopting the Agile mindset will help you immensely with applying Scrum and solving everyday problems with your projects. We then introduced the Scrum framework, describing its three components and we reviewed its benefits, namely its flexibility, adaptability, and transparency. Finally, we examined the iterative and incremental development approach used by Scrum and highlighted its relevance to the modern software development world.

We concluded the chapter by talking about PSM assessments and the PSM I exam. Throughout the rest of this book, we will expand our knowledge on Scrum and how to apply it, thereby gaining knowledge that will help you to obtain your PMS I certificate and become a successful practicing Scrum Master.

In the next chapter, we will discuss the Scrum values and principles and how they support and affect the Scrum framework.

Further reading

- *Principles behind the Agile Manifesto*, `https://agilemanifesto.org/principles.html`

- *Scrum Values meet Agile Principles*, `https://www.scrum.org/resources/blog/scrum-values-meet-agile-principles`

- *The State of Agile*, `https://betanews.com/2019/05/07/state-of-agile-report`

- *The Scrum Guide*, `https://www.scrumguides.org/docs/scrumguide/v2017/2017-Scrum-Guide-US.pdf`

- Ken Schwaber and Jeff Sutherland, *Software in 30 Days: How Agile Managers Beat the Odds, Delight Their Customers, and Leave Competitors in the Dust*, Wiley publications, 1st ed., Mar 2012

2
Scrum Theory and Principles

In this chapter, we will learn about the principles and values behind Scrum. At this point, you may be thinking *Hold on, Scrum is a practical, agile approach to software development, so why should I care about theory?* The simple answer here is that Scrum isn't a step-by-step process. It doesn't prescribe that you should follow step 1 and then step 2 and then maybe step 3 or 4. Scrum is a process *framework*. It tells us what we should value, what is important, sets out some rules, and gives us directions on how to apply these rules to achieve the things we value. Without knowing the underlying philosophy and principles, it is impossible to follow the directions Scrum sets out for us. So, with this in mind, this chapter is about the philosophy of Scrum, the empirical approach it is based on, its values, and its principles. We will cover the following topics in particular:

- The foundation of Scrum
- The pillars of empiricism
- The Scrum values
- The House of Scrum

By the end of this chapter, you will have learned what empiricism is and why it is important in software development. You will also know the pillars of empiricism and how they apply to Scrum, as well as knowing about the values of Scrum and how to apply them within the development process. We will round up the chapter with a short quiz that will allow you to test your newly found knowledge.

The foundation of Scrum

Scrum is founded on an empirical process theory of knowledge, or **empiricism**. Empiricism is derived from the Greek word *Empeiria*, that is, experience. It is the theory that all knowledge should be based on, and justified by, practical experience. Learning is based on our observations, perception, and experience gained from practice. Empiricism is often contrasted with **rationalism**, another theory of knowledge that regards reason as the chief source and standard of knowledge. In other words, rationalism determines truth based on the adoption of and adherence to intellectual templates and standards. Empiricism, on the other hand, determines truth based on the results of experimentation, evaluation of evidence, and its alignment with a perceived useful outcome.

At this point, you're probably asking yourself *What has this philosophical stuff got to do with software development?* Allow me to use a simple thought experiment:

Alice is managing a widget factory. She has 10 workers on the assembly line, and they are producing 10 widgets every day. During the holiday period, market demand for widgets goes up. The factory needs to start producing 20 widgets per day. Alice can see the solution: if 10 workers produce 10 widgets per day, then 20 workers will be producing 20 widgets a day. Alice doesn't need to put this to the test; it's a simple deduction based on mathematical axioms, inherently accepted as correct. So, Alice simply goes and hires 10 more workers. Problem solved.

Alice followed a **rationalist approach** and it worked. Now, let's imagine that Alice is managing a team of 10 software developers instead of factory widget makers. If Alice wants to double the team's productivity, can she simply do it by doubling the number of software developers?

The answer is of course not; any such suggestion would simply be laughable. Any experienced software professional can tell us that doubling the number of developers does not equate to a doubling of productivity. But why is that so? The reason is that, unlike widget-making, software development is a **non-deterministic process**. What that means is that following the same process, techniques, and standards will not necessarily produce the same results every single time. So, if Alice wants to double her team's productivity, she will probably need to hire some new developers, re-train some of the existing ones, re-assign some others, or apply different permutations of similar corrective actions. She will need to be monitoring the productivity effect of each of these actions and she'll need to be doing that constantly until she reaches the desired productivity increase. In short, Alice will need to follow an empirical approach in order to succeed.

Non-deterministic processes, such as software development, lend themselves very well to empiricism. Scrum provides multiple and frequent points for inspection and adaptation during the development process, thereby ensuring that any mistakes are caught and corrected early and that any requirement changes are adopted and integrated in plenty of time to avoid these accumulating and becoming detrimental to the system users. This constant application of inspection and adaptation, alongside transparency, is commonly known as the **pillars of empiricism**.

The pillars of empiricism

Just like a house needs pillars in order to be supported and withstand bad weather or earthquakes, so does a development framework need pillars to support it and make it resistant to adverse effects. For an empirical approach, such as Scrum, these pillars are **Inspection**, **Adaptation**, and **Transparency**.

The pillars of empiricism are summarized in the following diagram:

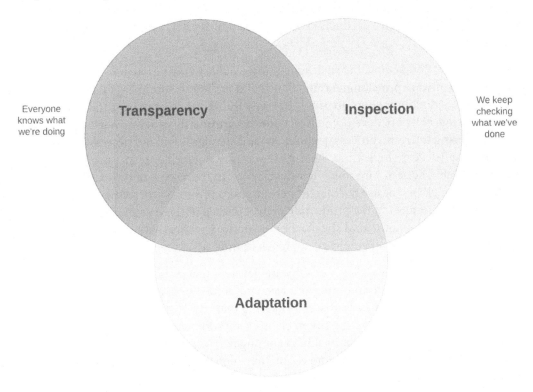

Figure 2.1 – The pillars of empiricism

Let's examine what each of these pillars means.

Inspection

As mentioned in *Chapter 1*, *Introduction to Scrum*, Scrum Teams produce certain artifacts. According to the *Scrum Guide*, Scrum practitioners should inspect Scrum Artifacts when these are being produced. **Inspections** should be honest and thorough, but they should not take over or obstruct the development work.

We have actually already mentioned one of these artifacts: the **Increment**. Increments, as well as the other artifacts that we'll examine in later chapters, are frequently inspected during Scrum. Even more importantly, the Scrum Team itself is open to inspection both as a collective and also among its members.

Inspection is about asking the right questions, such as the following:

- *Which practices that were followed did not work well?*

- *What are the things we did right in the Sprint?*

- *What could we have done better?*

Scrum fosters constant inspection of artifacts through the attendance of events, such as the **Daily Scrum**, the **Sprint Review**, and the **Sprint Retrospective**. We shall be closely examining these events in *Chapter 4, Scrum Events*.

Adaptation

Adaptation is a natural consequence of Inspection. In fact, Adaptation cannot exist without Inspection. During Inspection, we learn things. We learn what we did right and what we did wrong, how circumstances or requirements have changed, why some things worked, and why some things didn't. Adaptation is about responding to these learnings. It's about making changes so that things that failed can succeed next time round but also so that things that went well can go even better. These changes don't always have to be technical, such as using different technologies, for instance. They may also be personal, such as committing to more honesty and openness, or even environmental, such as requesting a break-out area in the office or an ergonomic keyboard.

Responding to change is one of the four values of the Agile Manifesto. Adaptation is the application of this value. The same Scrum Events that allow introspection also encourage adaptation. Events such as the Sprint Review give us the opportunity to take corrective actions and make plans. Scrum does not tell us how to take action or how to create plans. That's up to the Team. Scrum is a framework, not a process. It just sets the rules and creates opportunities to inspect and adapt. The rest is up to us.

Transparency

In order to be able to inspect and adapt, we need to be able to easily observe what we do and understand how and why we do it. To achieve that, we must make our events, artifacts, and the team itself open to inspection. This is what **Transparency** is all about: exposing our way of working, our actions, and our thinking to the team and stakeholders.

Transparency must be exercised across all three Scrum components: the team, the events, and the artifacts. There are specific ways in which Transparency can be applied in each of the components:

- **Scrum Team**: When the team starts working on a Sprint, they make the Sprint Goal visible to all stakeholders. This can be done by simply using a whiteboard at a place where everyone can see it or maybe using something more sophisticated such as a wiki or online collaboration tool. As the team works through the Sprint, its progress is also made visible to the stakeholders. Using a Scrum Board and burndown charts helps to achieve this. We'll talk more about these in *Chapter 6, Planning and Estimating with Scrum*.

- **Events**: As mentioned when we discussed Inspection and Adaptation, Scrum Events – such as the Sprint Review and the Sprint Retrospective – allow us to make changes, take actions, and create plans. These changes, actions, and plans must be visible to all stakeholders. How we do this is up to us; we may want to use specific tooling or just plain old email. The important thing here is that, whichever way we use it, the outcome of the Scrum Events is visible to all.

- **Artifacts**: Scrum has a number of artifacts such as the Product and Sprint Backlog (more on these in *Chapter 5, Scrum Artifacts*) that serve as information capture devices throughout the Scrum cycle. This information must be made clearly visible and understood by the team and all stakeholders. The visibility and availability of this information are crucial in making product-critical decisions.

Now that we've understood what the three pillars of Scrum mean, lett's examine the values that help support them.

The Scrum values

Just like the pillars of a house are built with concrete, iron, and stone, so do the Scrum pillars need material to build them with. This material is the ethical values of **commitment**, **courage**, **focus**, **openness**, and **respect**. The Scrum values may be easier to remember visually:

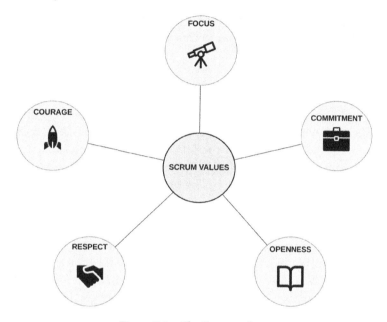

Figure 2.2 – The Scrum values

Only when these values are adopted by the whole team can the pillars of Inspection, Adaptation, and Transparency become strong enough to support and protect the team and the development process. Successful use of Scrum depends on people applying and constantly honing these values. Let's take a closer look at each of these:

- **Commitment** is about committing ourselves to the team and the Sprint Goal. It means that we are prepared to help the team achieve the goal, even though we may not personally agree with the goal or any design or architectural decisions made in its pursuit. Once the team has agreed on the tasks to be completed in a Sprint, we commit ourselves to finishing those tasks. Commitment docs not mean that we blindly accept any decision made by others and follow them unquestionably; it does mean however that once our questions have been answered and our doubts communicated to the team, we commit ourselves to the decided direction and goals. As Scrum Masters, we foster commitment by preventing mid-Sprint changes and removing any impediments that may prevent the team from committing to a task or a goal.

- **Courage** means that we are willing to accept when we are wrong or when our opinion does not align with the direction the team is going in. None of us are perfect, we all make mistakes, and – as the saying goes – it takes a brave person to admit their mistakes. Courage also means that we are prepared to have difficult conversations if need be. Courage does not mean being disparaging of other people's opinions, being argumentative, or pushing back against the consensus. As Scrum Masters, courage also means that we stand up to other stakeholders when they try to sidetrack the team from the Sprint Goal or when they try to undermine Scrum practices or principles.

- **Focus** is about keeping certain things in mind as high-importance items and finishing what we start. In the short term, our focus should be on achieving the Sprint Goal. In the longer term, our focus should be on delivering the product our customers need, while applying the Scrum values and supporting the pillars of Scrum. Scrum Masters encourage focus by encouraging full team participation at the daily Scrum meeting and helping the team define and adhere to the definition of **Done** (more on this in *Chapter 6, Planning and Estimating with Scrum*).

- **Openness** is about being upfront and honest about what we do. We all come across issues and challenges that prevent us from completing our tasks. Being open means that we let the team know about them. It's better for the team to know about such things early than the customer finding out about them later on. Being open means presenting new ideas to the team and discussing them, rather than keeping them to ourselves. Openness also means that when we present an idea or design, we talk about its drawbacks as well as its advantages. Openness does not mean that we keep reminding everyone about our achievements or brag about our skills. Scrum Masters foster an open environment by encouraging team members to talk about any issues and ensuring constructive feedback from stakeholders is accessible to all team members.

- **Respect** is more about treating others with respect, rather than trying to earn it. Being respectful means that we consider other people's ideas and suggestions and if we disagree, we provide constructive criticism and reasoned arguments, instead of patronizingly dismissing them. Respect means recognizing that different people have different skillsets; some people will be better at something than us, while others will be worse. It means recognizing that people come from different backgrounds and will look at the same problem from different perspectives to our own. Last, but not least, we need to keep in mind that we are all human; we all make bad decisions, have bad days, and occasionally achieve great things. Respect is about recognizing and accepting this simple fact. Scrum Masters promote respect by encouraging the discussion of new ideas, instead of their dismissal. They encourage constructive feedback, instead of criticism. They promote collective team action to address shortcomings, rather than personal judgment and punitive actions.

The Scrum values can also be thought of as the bricks we use when building a house. The house builders apply bricks, one on top of another, to make a solid wall. Similarly, the Scrum Team needs to be applying the Scrum values daily in order to build a solid product. Let's explore this metaphor a bit more…

The House of Scrum

A good way to visualize Scrum is as a house. A house needs a foundation, and for Scrum, the foundation is empiricism. The pillars that support the house are Adaptation, Inspection, and Transparency. The walls are constructed with bricks, which are made of the Scrum values. We can visualize this like so:

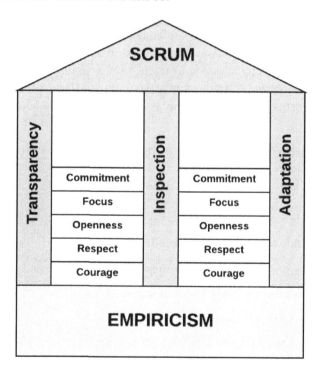

Figure 2.3 – The House of Scrum

As with any other house, if the foundation is taken away, the house will collapse. If the pillars crumble, the roof will fall in. If the walls are damaged, the house will be exposed to the elements. The preceding metaphor helps us visualize the theoretical underpinning of Scrum, as well as the importance of making Scrum a whole and usable process framework.

Summary

In this chapter, we described the empirical foundation of Scrum, its underlying pillars, and the Scrum values. We also explained how these principles and values come together to form a solid process framework.

You should know by now why empiricism is an ideal approach for software development, what the pillars of empiricism are, what the Scrum values mean, and how they can be practiced in everyday life.

We learned about empiricism, which is a fitting way of approaching software development. In fact, an empirical approach of observation and experimentation underpins the scientific method that has provided our civilization with the quality of life and technological advances we now enjoy. Similarly, the pillars of empiricism (Transparency, Inspection, Adaptation) not only help us understand and apply Scrum but they can also be very helpful in many other aspects of our professional life. Finally, the Scrum values are essential in making Scrum add value to our team. They help us understand how to apply the Scrum rules and ceremonies in the right spirit and treat them as improvement and communication opportunities instead of things that we have to do because Scrum dictates it.

In the next chapter, we will be getting into the basics of Scrum by starting to examine the Scrum Team and its roles, so stay tuned for that.

Questions

1. Which of the following statements best describes Scrum?

    a) Scrum is the most popular development process.

    b) Scrum is one of many Agile methodologies.

    c) Scrum is an Agile process framework.

    d) Scrum prescribes an Agile development process.

2. During my development process, I constantly take actions, measure their effects, and adjust my next actions accordingly. Which theory-of-knowledge approach underpins my development process?

    a) Rationalism

    b) Realism

    c) Empiricism

    d) Pragmatism

3. Bob, a Scrum Team member, has presented a new design to the team, however, he neglected to mention that the new design will not work under certain conditions. Which Scrum value has Bob not adhered to?

    a) Commitment

    b) Courage

    c) Focus

    d) Openness

    e) Respect

4. Alice, a Scrum Team member working on a Sprint task, designs a new algorithm to help implement a task and presents it to the team. After careful consideration, other team members suggest the use of a different algorithm, better suited to the specific task. Alice uses the newly suggested algorithm and completes the task successfully. Which Scrum values did Alice demonstrate?

    a) Focus and respect

    b) Openness and commitment

    c) Courage and loyalty

    d) None of the above

5. During a Sprint, Carol – a Scrum Team member – is approached by the company CTO and asked whether she can help with a non-product-related problem. Carol stops working on her Sprint tasks for 1 day and solves the CTO's problem. She then resumes working on the Sprint and completes her tasks successfully. Which statement best describes Carol's action?

    a) A heroic action that managed to help a senior company member, while still achieving the Sprint commitment. Carol should be rewarded.

    b) Carol should have asked her manager's permission before helping the CTO.

    c) Carol should have let the team know that she would stop working on Sprint tasks for a day. Still, the Sprint tasks were completed in the end, so no harm was done.

    d) Carol did not live by the Scrum value of focus.

3
The Scrum Team

In the previous chapter, we discussed the Scrum principles and values. In this chapter, we'll talk about the parts that make up the Scrum framework, starting with the Scrum Team. In this chapter, we'll learn all about the members of the Scrum Team, what their roles and responsibilities are and how they interact with each other. In addition, we'll answer some questions often asked about the Scrum Team that are not adequately covered in the Scrum Guide. By the end of the chapter, you should know exactly what each team role should and shouldn't be doing. Specifically, we'll be covering the following topics:

- Identifying a Scrum Team
- Introducing the Scrum Master
- Working with the Product Owner
- Getting acquainted with the Developers

Let's begin by understanding what makes a Scrum Team special.

Identifying a Scrum Team

The Scrum Team is a small group of people who work together to deliver a software solution or product to a client. The Scrum Team consists of three specific roles, a **Product Owner**, a **Scrum Master**, and **Developers**. The Scrum Team is a cohesive unit of professionals focused on delivering a product. The team is responsible for performing any and all product-related activities needed in order to achieve the Product Goal. They are empowered by the organization to manage their own work.

Scrum Teams differ from traditional software teams. Before Agile became a *thing*, software project teams would consist of a number of software developers working within well-defined boundaries and within a strict hierarchy of duties and responsibilities. Traditionally, business analysts would communicate with the stakeholder and capture requirements. These would then be passed to the developers. The software system's architecture and high-level design would be established in advance by the technical lead or solution architect and then developers would implement the design and deliver the software. Finally, the delivered code would be tested by a separate **Quality Assurance** (**QA**) team, who would then accept the delivery or raise issues, as appropriate.

The whole process would be supervised by a project manager who would – among other things – allocate tasks and manage the project schedule, team members, and project resources. The team, or teams, managed by the project manager could vary in size from a handful of people to many dozens, depending on the company and the project.

This structure was well-suited to a linear and cascading development and delivery lifecycle, known as the **waterfall** lifecycle, where requirements were rigid and client involvement was low (see *The value of an iterative and incremental approach section in Chapter 1, Introduction to Scrum*). However, as software technologies began to expand and the internet era dawned, it became painfully obvious that this model was not viable. Software became ubiquitous in people's lives, competition for software products increased, and clients started to crave flexibility, adaptability, and bigger involvement in the products they were paying the software industry to create. Scrum offered a new development and delivery model and the first thing to change was the structure of the software team, by identifying three distinct roles (Product Owner, Scrum Master, and Developers). The other thing that set a Scrum Team apart was certain characteristics that the team possessed. Let's talk about these characteristics for a minute.

Defining a Scrum Team

As mentioned, the Scrum Team consists of a Product Owner, the Developers, and a Scrum Master. This structure is designed to optimize flexibility, creativity, and productivity. But a Scrum Team is more than just its structure; it has certain unique characteristics too:

- **Scrum Teams are self-managing**: That means the team decides between themselves how to best accomplish their work, instead of relying on external direction.

- **Scrum Teams are cross-functional**: That means they have all the skills and competencies necessary to deliver the required software, without the need for external specialists or consultants.

- **Scrum Teams are numerically bounded**: The Scrum Team should consist of no more than 10 members in order to optimize productivity and minimize coordination complexity.

- **Scrum Teams differentiate between the product, the work, and the process**: There is no project manager who supervises all three. The Product Owner looks after the product, the Developers look after themselves and the required work, and the Scrum Master looks after the process while facilitating the rest of the team.

The following diagram visualizes the roles within the Scrum Team:

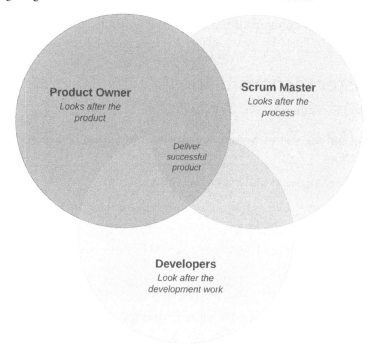

Figure 3.1 – The Scrum Team roles

Every role, depicted as a circle in the diagram, has its own area of responsibility. However, the circles largely intersect one another, denoting the communication and collaboration taking place between the team members, in their respective roles. There is an area of the diagram where the three roles intersect each other. This is what is necessary for the team to function productively and deliver the product successfully; in Scrum, the team must often come together and make collective decisions. Scrum prescribes separation of responsibilities but also encourages and promotes collective action and accountability.

Now that we know how the Scrum Team is structured, let's take a look at the specific roles and their responsibilities, starting with the Scrum Master.

Introducing the Scrum Master

The **Scrum Master** role is one of the most misunderstood concepts of Scrum. Many people find it hard to understand the value of someone with no apparent authority or influence on the product or the team. However, the Scrum Master role is crucial for a team's success. The Scrum Master is often referred to as a servant-leader, and this is for good reason. They are the person who ensures that the team is working well together, that impediments to progress are quickly removed, and that the team is moving efficiently toward its goal. They interact with the rest of the Scrum Team but also with the organization and stakeholders. In this section, we'll learn about the things a Scrum Master should do, the things they shouldn't do, and we'll answer some commonly asked questions about this role.

Scrum Master responsibilities

The Scrum Master is responsible for the following:

- Promoting and supporting Scrum as defined in the Scrum Guide (see the *Further reading* section)

- Helping the organization understand and enact Scrum

- Ensuring that Scrum Events take place at the appropriate time and that they are time-boxed

- Ensuring that the purpose and value of Scrum Events is well understood by the Scrum Team

- Ensuring that Scrum Events are conducted in a positive and constructive manner

- Removing impediments to the Developers' progress

- Helping provide transparency for Scrum Artifacts

- Coaching the Developers on how to increase self-management, cross-functionality, and productivity

- Helping stakeholders in their interactions with the Scrum Team

- Coaching and advising the organization on Scrum adoption techniques and practices

- Coaching the Product Owner on effective Product Backlog management techniques.

It's obvious that the Scrum Master has a widely scoped role that fosters interactions within and without the Scrum Team. Their overarching responsibility is to ensure that the Scrum rules are applied correctly, the Scrum principles are applied, and its values are respected. In addition, the Scrum Team facilitates the Scrum by providing coaching and guidance.

Things outside the Scrum Master realm

The Scrum Master is someone who facilitates, rather than directs. They enable, instead of coercing. They advise, but do not dictate. Here are some of the things Scrum Masters are *not responsible* for:

- Product development, such as telling the Developers how to turn Product Backlog items into deliverable pieces of functioning code. The Developers are self-managing. However, the Scrum Master can advise them on how to be more productive or cross-functional.

- Product management, such as telling the Product Owner what to include in the Product Backlog or which items should be prioritized. However, the Scrum Master can advise the Product Owner on how to create clear and concise backlog items or suggest techniques for prioritizing items in the backlog.

- People management, such as employer performance reviews, time management, and similar activities.

In short, the Scrum Master has authority over the process, but not the people or product.

A good way of thinking about the Scrum Master is like a personal coach at the gym. They can tell you how to do the exercises correctly, how to adjust the equipment, and they can motivate you towards reaching your training goal. But they cannot make you perform the exercises unless you want to do them. The personal coach is there to facilitate and enable your training regime and help you reach your goals. In a similar fashion, the Scrum Master is there to facilitate and enable the Scrum Team and help them reach their goals.

Scrum Master Q&A

- **Q**: Can the Scrum Master also be a Developer?

  A: Yes, this is not prohibited. In fact, it's not an uncommon occurrence. If you judge that the project and the team's composition allow for a Scrum Master to also be a developer, that is fine. However, you should be aware of the risks. There may be a conflict of demands, for instance, effort for a development task may be required at the same time as effort to clear a team impediment. The credibility of the Scrum Master may also be undermined, as they are supposed to be protecting the Developers from outside interference, which may be interpreted to be for personal reasons if the Scrum Master is also a Developer. As a rule of thumb, assigning the role of Scrum Master and Developer to the same person should be done as a last resort.

- **Q**: Should the same Scrum Master remain with the Scrum Team for the duration of the project?

  A: Changes in the Scrum Team membership, indeed in any team, can be disruptive. Because the Scrum Master role is so influential and cross-cutting, changing the Scrum Master mid-project can cause great disruption on many levels. It is something to be avoided, unless absolutely necessary.

- **Q**: Can the same Scrum Master be someone external to the organization, such as a consultant/contractor?

  A: Yes, they can. It is often beneficial to hire an experienced Scrum Master from outside, especially if the organization is just starting their Agile journey and need someone to guide and direct them. However, in the long term, it is prudent for the organization to cultivate native Scrum Masters that they can apply to different teams and projects.

Let's now take a look at what the role of the Product Owner is.

Working with the Product Owner

While the Scrum Master helps the team move efficiently towards their goals, the Product Owner ensures that these goals are valid and beneficial. They set the vision and goals of the project. They are responsible for maximizing the value of the product based on the work of the Developers. Let's take a look at what a Product Owner should do, what they shouldn't do, and let's get some answers to some commonly asked questions about this role.

Product Owner responsibilities

The Product Owner is responsible for the following:

- Managing the Product Backlog. This includes adding or removing items, ordering and prioritizing items, and ensuring that the backlog is visible and available to the Scrum Team and to stakeholders.

- Ensuring items in the backlog are clearly understood by the Developers, to a level that they can use the items to produce working code.

- Monitoring and assessing progress towards the stated goals and product delivery and making this information available to stakeholders.

- Identifying the required objectives for the Sprint.

- Deciding whether a Product Increment is usable enough to be released.

- Canceling a Sprint. This should happen only if sudden and extraordinary circumstances render the Sprint Goal untenable. It should be a very rare event.

Overall, the Product Owner is someone who's facing in two directions: inwards and outwards. They need to interact with clients and stakeholders in order to best understand the product's needs and its position within the market. They also need to interact with the Developers in order to communicate these needs and express them as clear and concise Product Backlog items.

Things outside the Product Owner realm

As you can see, the Product Owner's responsibilities are very well defined. The product is their primary concern. Product Owners are *not responsible* for the following:

- Estimating the amount of work needed to deliver Product Backlog items. The Product Owner may help the Developers to better understand the business process or domain complexity inherent in a backlog item, but the Developers are solely responsible for the estimates.

- Setting the Sprint Goal. This is accomplished by the Scrum Team as a whole. The Product Backlog may, however, identify the immediate objectives needed in order to align the work with the product vision or roadmap.

- Creating the Sprint Backlog, that is the set of items targeted for the Sprint. The Developers ultimately decide which items should go in the Sprint Backlog, based on their capacity and estimates. The Product Backlog may provide input as to the items most likely needed to achieve the Sprint Goal.

- Modifying the Sprint Backlog during the Sprint. Only the Developers can do that. The Product Backlog may interfere with the Sprint only in the unlikely event that the Sprint Goal cannot be reached, and the Sprint needs to be canceled.

- Interfering with the Developers in any way, shape, or form, such as incentivizing individuals or resolving conflicts.

It is very clear that the Product Owner's remit begins and ends with the product. The process and development work are outside their sphere of influence.

Product Owner Q&A

- **Q**: Should the Product Owner be answering all questions about the product and Product Backlog items?

  A: The Product Owner is responsible for clarifying the backlog items and clearly communicating the product's requirements. This doesn't mean that they must be personally answering every single question, but it means that they are responsible for having the questions answered. It is not unusual for the Product Owner to refer a Developer to a client-side stakeholder or other subject matter expert in order to provide clarification. Sometimes, a Product Owner may even refer to another similar product or website and indicate that the feature in question should *work like that*. This is all fine as long as it ensures that questions are answered clearly and that Product Backlog items are unambiguous.

- **Q**: Can the Product Owner set deadlines?

  A: The Product Owner needs to deliver value to the organization by means of delivering the Product in a timely manner. They are well within their rights to provide a product roadmap and set milestones and goals. For instance, it's perfectly reasonable for a Product Owner to say, *we need to deliver features X and Y within 6 months, to hit the market before a competitor's rival product*. What they must not do, however, is to pressurize the team to increase their effort or change their way of working in order to reach that deadline. It is up to the Developers to plan their work in the way they see fit and to raise concerns when planning. For example, in looking to plan sprints in such a way that the required features are delivered within a deadline, the team may identify the need for adding more developers to it. This should then be raised with the Scrum Master as a potential impediment. Also, everyone should keep in mind that Scrum is an empirical process. Every Sprint helps increase our understanding of the domain and of our capacity to deliver working software. Therefore, deciding 6 months in advance whether some features will be delivered by that time is not a pragmatic or sensible approach and is not aligned with the Agile principles (see *What is Agile software development? section in Chapter 1, Introduction to Scrum*). It is the Scrum Master's responsibility to ensure that this is well understood by everyone.

- **Q**: Can the Product Owner role be performed by more than one person?

  A: The answer is kind of yes but no. The organization may decide that there should be a team of product and domain specialists to drive the product forward. That is absolutely fine. However, as far as the Scrum Team is concerned, there should be only one person representing that product team, that is the Product Owner. They should be the only person directly interacting with the rest of the Scrum Team. The reason for this is that dealing with a committee nearly always increases communication paths and the time needed to clarify or answer questions. So, having a product team is fine as long as it is invisible to the Scrum Team. There should only be one source of truth concerning the product and that is the Product Owner.

Finally, it's time to learn about one more role within the Scrum Team.

Getting acquainted with the Developers

The Developers are a cross-functional, self-managing group that is responsible for converting Sprint Backlog items into working, releasable code. In this section, we'll learn about the Developer responsibilities, the things outside their realm, and we'll answer some commonly asked questions about this role.

The Developers are self-managing

Self-management means that they are responsible for making decisions about the work they are doing and about the way they function. There is no hierarchy among the Developers. No team member can tell another team member what to do. Disagreements must be resolved with discussions and consensus-forming. Traditionally, developers have been structured according to seniority and skillsets. The most senior developers would be making the decisions. Work would be split according to areas of expertise, for instance, the frontend expert would work on the UI, the testing expert would do the testing, and so on. This can still happen between Scrum Team Developers with consent, but it cannot be mandated. It may only happen organically with the team's input and acceptance. So the team may decide that a single person will be doing all testing work. This is fine, as long as the whole team has discussed and agreed to it. Self-management means that such decisions are not dictated by people outside the group. Furthermore, the Developers own all the work collectively, even if there is one person doing it. Self-managing groups are empowered and apply collective responsibility, that is, the whole group is responsible for any decision or action taken by any one group member.

The Developers are a cross-functional group

A **cross-functional** group is a group that has all the necessary skills and capabilities required to turn backlog items into working, deliverable code. These skills and capabilities will differ depending on the domain and the project the team is working on. A project that involves transitioning a system to the cloud will require a much wider DevOps skillset than, say, a data management project. Conversely, a data management project will require a team with a strong business domain and analytical skills, rather than DevOps. A cross-functional team should have adequate skills to deliver what is needed to realize the product's goals and vision. This fosters a collective-ownership approach. Any team member can work on any task and there is no *pass-the-buck* blame mentality in the team.

A common mistake many organizations make when creating Scrum Teams is to create a generic group of Developers. These teams will typically have a frontend expert, a backend expert, a database expert, and so on. Standardizing teams in such a way means that you risk compromising the efficiency and productivity of the team. If the product is frontend heavy, for example, then having just one team member with frontend skills will ensure other members without the necessary level of knowledge will be required to perform more complex frontend tasks more often. This is not a bad thing in itself, but it will impact the team's velocity (see *qs*) and may tempt the organization to call for external expert help or make staff changes, which will gravely disrupt the team. Developers should be selected around the product and each Developer group should have a unique sum of skills and knowledge, which will allow it to perform its function autonomously and independently.

Developer structure

A Scrum Team consists of up to 10 members. According to the *Scrum Guide*, larger teams are less productive and communicate more poorly. Taking into account the Product Owner and the Scrum Master, that means that a Scrum Team should include no more than 8 developers. On the other hand, fewer than 3 developers are likely to not have the necessary skill-set to deliver working software and may also have reduced productivity.

Developers within the Scrum Team have no titles, though they may have different skills and experience levels. Everyone has an equal voice within the team.

The Scrum Team Developers should remain together for as long possible, even outside the duration of the current project. The longer the team remains together, the more efficient and effective it becomes. Changes in the team composition will affect its cohesion and productivity.

Developer responsibilities

Developers are responsible for performing the work needed to provide a Product Increment, that is, a body of Done and deliverable work. In detail, they are responsible for the following:

- Attending the Daily Scrum (see *Chapter 4, Scrum Events*).

- Meeting after the Daily Scrum, to discuss, plan, or adapt the rest of the work required for the Sprint.

- Changing items in the Sprint Backlog during a Sprint, if needed.

- Collaborating with the Product Owner to define the Sprint Backlog.

- Attending the Sprint Planning meeting to help plan for the Sprint. This includes monitoring the team's capacity and estimating Product Backlog items.

- Define **Done** (see *Chapter 6, Planning and Estimating with Scrum*), if not already defined by the organization, and communicate its definition to the rest of the Scrum Team.

In short, Developers have full authority over what work they are doing and how they are doing it.

Things outside the Developers' realm

Developers are *not responsible* for the following:

- Deciding what items should go in the Product Backlog. This is the Product Owner's responsibility.

- Responding to work requests from people outside the Scrum Team. Such requests should be re-directed to the Product Owner.

- Releasing software to the stakeholders. Developers are responsible for producing a Done Product Increment at each Sprint. It is up to the Product Owner to decide if and when the increment will be released.

In summary, the Developers have full control over the work needed to create and release the product, but not over the product itself.

Developer Q&A

In this section, we'll tackle some pragmatic questions about Developers that are not covered in the Scrum Guide. However, these are questions that are frequently asked by stakeholders and Scrum Teams alike:

- **Q**: For the team to be cross-functional, should the team members all be good generalists?

  A: Not necessarily. The most efficient Scrum Team Developers are a mix of good generalists and specialists. Having only generalists risks the team missing some specialized knowledge or skills when they need it most. On the other hand, a team of only specialists inevitably leads to silos within the team, inhibiting collaboration and collective responsibility.

- **Q**: Who selects the Developers for a Scrum Team?

  A: This is a loaded question. The generic answer is that this is up to the organization the team belongs to. If the organization is new to Scrum, then management will have to select a number of developers they think have the right skills to crew a cross-functional team. If the organization already has a Scrum Master, then they should be coaching them on the best way to achieve that. Now, if the organization has already embraced Scrum and just needs to create a team for a new project, then the most Agile way of doing that would be to allow the currently available developers to decide between themselves, with a Scrum Master's guidance, who should be in the new Scrum Team. Ultimately, the authority over the Scrum Team's resourcing lies with the organization.

- **Q**: Who's responsible for resolving conflicts between Developers?

  A: The team is self-managing and that includes the responsibility to resolve internal disagreements or conflicts. The Scrum Master should coach the team in conflict-resolution techniques and the Agile mindset, where necessary. If the conflict cannot be resolved and it hinders productivity or collaboration, then it should be raised as an impediment for the Scrum Master to deal with.

We have now covered all three roles within the Scrum Team.

Summary

In this chapter, we learned how a Scrum Team operates and in which ways it is different from traditional project teams. We discussed the roles of Scrum Master, Product Owner, and Developer and defined their areas of responsibility. For Scrum to succeed, it is essential that everyone understands their role within the team and also the extent and limits of their authority and responsibility, which is why we also discussed some of the boundaries each team role has.

Finally, we addressed some common, real-life issues faced by Scrum Teams that aren't fully addressed in the Scrum Guide. We did this in the form of a Q&A session for each role. All this should form a solid basis for understanding how Scrum works. The knowledge gained here about the Scrum Team will be solidified in the next chapter, where we will be exploring Scrum Events.

Questions

1. At the end of the last sprint, the Developers shipped software that was not working as intended. The Scrum Master suggests that, in the next sprint, the most senior developer should review all code before it is released. Which one of the following statements best reflects this action?

    a) It's a good idea. It will reduce the risk of shipping defective software again.

    b) It's a bad idea. The senior developer should not spend all their time reviewing code.

    c) It's up to the Product Owner to complain if defective software was shipped.

    d) The Scrum Master has no place telling the Developers how to deliver working software.

2. During the last two sprints, the Developers failed to complete all the items in the Sprint Backlog. Which is the most appropriate thing for the Scrum Master to say?

    a) The team should start work earlier in the morning, so they can get more done.

    b) The team should consider increasing the sprint duration.

    c) Team members who don't pull their weight should be replaced.

    d) The team should tell the Product Owner that they cannot cope with so many items in the Product Backlog.

3. Which statement best describes a Product Owner's responsibility?

    a) Directing the Developers.

    b) Optimizing the value of the work the Developers do.

    c) Managing the project and ensuring that the work meets the commitments to the stakeholders.

    d) Keeping stakeholders from distracting the Developers.

4. Who has the final say on the order of the Product Backlog?

    a) The Product Owner

    b) The Scrum Master

    c) The Developers

    d) The stakeholders

5. Lisa, a Developer is working on a feature but is unclear as to exactly how that feature should work. What should Lisa do?

    a) Tell the Scrum Master she has an impediment.

    b) Make some assumptions about the functionality and get it done.

    c) Ask another Developer.

    d) Ask the Product Owner.

6. Developers within a Scrum Team should change:

    a) Never, because it reduces productivity.

    b) As needed, with no special allowance for changes in productivity.

    c) As needed, while taking into account a short-term reduction in productivity.

    d) Every Sprint, to promote shared learning.

7. Who is responsible for managing the progress of work during a Sprint?

    a) The Product Owner

    b) The most senior member of the team

    c) The Scrum Master

    d) The Developers

4
Scrum Events

In the previous chapter, we learned all about the **Scrum Team**. In this chapter, we'll discuss another important aspect of Scrum: **Scrum Events**. These are regularly occurring events, intended to promote transparency and inspection (see *The pillars of empiricism section in Chapter 2, Scrum Theory and Principles*). They are time-boxed events, meaning that they have a maximum duration. These events are as follows:

- The Sprint
- Sprint Planning
- Daily Scrum
- Sprint Review
- Sprint Retrospective

We are going to learn what each event entails, why it is beneficial to the Scrum Team, and how it should be conducted. In detail, we'll cover the following topics:

- Getting ready to Sprint
- Starting the Sprint with Sprint Planning
- Keeping on the right track with the Daily Scrum
- Inspecting the product during the Sprint Review
- Inspecting the team with the Sprint Retrospective

By the end of the chapter, you'll have learned how to create a Sprint Goal and a Definition of Done, how to plan for the Sprint, what to do during the Daily Scrum, and how to conduct the Sprint Review and Sprint Retrospective events.

Let's start with the event that's at the heart of Scrum: the Sprint.

Getting ready to Sprint

In *Chapter 1, Introduction to Scrum, in the The value of an iterative and incremental approach section*, we examined the concept of developing software in short iterations, where each iteration builds upon the working software provided by its predecessors. We call such an iteration a **Sprint**. A Sprint is a container event, as all the other Scrum Events take place within the duration and context of a Sprint. The ultimate purpose of the Sprint is to have the Developers produce an **Increment**. An Increment is a piece of *working and potentially shippable* software that leverages previous Increments. We'll talk more about what this means in a subsequent section. However, the Sprint also provides space and time for all the other Scrum Events, where the whole Scrum Team comes together to plan, inspect, and adapt. A good way to visualize the Sprint is as a cyclical process, demarcated by other events, as illustrated in the following diagram:

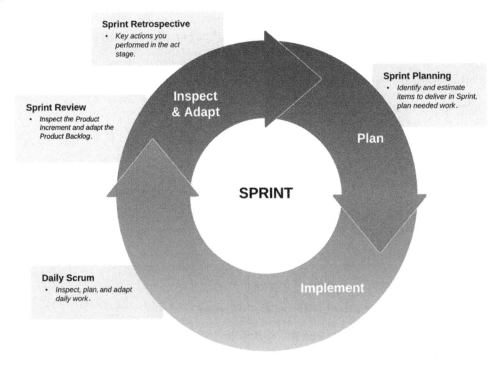

Figure 4.1 – The Sprint as an event container

Each Sprint begins with a planning phase. The is represented in Scrum by the **Sprint Planning** event. The implementation phase, where all the development work happens, is enabled by the **Daily Scrum** Event. Finally, the last phase of the Sprint (**Inspection & Adaptation**) is marked by two events, the **Sprint Review** and the **Sprint Retrospective**. In the next sections, we'll be discussing these events in great detail.

With that in mind, let's see what we need to do in order to start sprinting!

Deciding on the Sprint duration

A Sprint is time-boxed to a maximum duration of a calendar month. Most organizations choose to interpret this as 4 working weeks, as it's easier to organize recurring events by weeks rather than by calendar dates. The Scrum Guide does not specify a minimum length for the Sprint, although – for practical reasons – a duration of less than 1 week would not be realistic. Most Scrum Teams use a Sprint duration of 2-3 weeks. Once a Sprint starts, its duration cannot be changed.

Having short Sprints is a risk limitation strategy. By producing shippable code often, we are more likely to discover unfeasible requirements or technical dead-ends early, without having committed a large amount of time and effort. Having Sprints longer than a month would increase that risk.

Setting the Sprint Goal

The **Sprint Goal** is an objective meant to provide guidance and focus to the Developers. A Sprint Goal should add value by addressing risks, testing assumptions, or delivering features. It should be used to facilitate decision-making when deciding which work items to tackle in the Sprint. A good Sprint Goal will be something such as *Offer discounts to multi-buying customers*. This enhances the product's functionality and provides value to the client-side stakeholders by delivering a needed feature. It could also be *Create and test production pipeline*. This adds value to stakeholders by ensuring that we have a mechanism for releasing the product to our clients and it also addresses potential infrastructure and deployment risks.

When setting the Sprint Goal, the team should be asking these questions:

- *What value are we trying to deliver with this Sprint? And to whom?* Some Sprints may be focused solely on adding new features, while others may include some effort for code re-factoring or optimizations. The important point is to identify who benefits from the Sprint and how.

- *Is the goal reachable and realistic?* If the goal reaches for something that the Developers cannot deliver within a single Sprint, it will cause confusion and loss of morale among the team.

- *How do we know the goal has been met?* We need to identify some validation methods or criteria so that we can know whether the goal has been achieved. This could be as simple as asking a client stakeholder to test the Increment.

Having a good Sprint Goal helps the whole team focus and gives them confidence in delivering software, which adds testable value.

Defining Done as working and potentially shippable software

As mentioned at the start of the section, the aim of the Sprint is to produce an **Increment** of working and potentially shippable software. But what exactly does this mean? Let's find out.

The first indication of working software is software that has been *tested*. Testing works on multiple levels: unit, component, integration, and so on. Whatever our testing levels are, we must ensure that all tests are successful, before we can call our software *working*. Another indication of working and also potentially shippable software is that it *functions as specified*. Having a **specification** is very important. A specification is an agreement between us and our customer about how our system should function. Specifications written in **Behavior-Driven Development (BDD)** style (see the *Further reading section*) express system behavior in a clear and consistent manner. It then becomes easy to verify that our code enacts this behavior. This can take place either manually or by automated scripts. Many Scrum Teams not using BDD impose the addition of acceptance criteria on user stories the team is working on. Working and potentially shippable software should always pass those criteria.

Ultimately, it is down to each organization and team to define what they mean by *working and potentially shippable* software. The Scrum Guide states the following:

> *The purpose of each Sprint is to deliver Increments of potentially releasable functionality that adhere to the Scrum Team's current definition of "Done".*

For many teams, **Done** may mean that, as well as tested and functioning to specification, code has also been merged into a particular source repository branch or that it has been deployed successfully to a staging environment. The Definition of Done should fit the needs of each organization, team, and product. For instance, an organization may define **Done** to include coded, unit-tested, code-reviewed, checked in to master branch and integration-tested on the staging environment. Other organizations may choose to use different operational criteria for their own Definition of Done.

Important note

Do not take *potentially shippable* to mean the same as *shippable* software. Just because our Increment is "potentially shippable" does not mean that it will or should be shipped. Feature dependencies or marketing considerations may mean that it may not be wise to ship an Increment at the present moment. Further activities may be required in order to ship a *potentially shippable* Increment, such as system hardening or user training. It is up to the Product Owner, in consultation with the stakeholders, to decide whether an Increment should be shipped or not.

Now that we understand what the Sprint duration should be, what the Sprint Goal is about, and how to define Done, let's examine the rest of the Scrum Events, which all take place within the Sprint.

Starting the Sprint with Sprint Planning

Sprint Planning's purpose is to define the work to be performed during the Sprint. This plan is created by the collaborative work of the entire Scrum Team. The duration of the Sprint Planning should be no more than 8 hours for a 1-month Sprint. It should be proportionately shorter for shorter Sprints.

The Sprint Planning aims to answer two questions:

- What can be delivered in the Increment resulting from the upcoming Sprint? This is achieved by the Scrum Team estimating which Product Backlog items can be realistically delivered in the Sprint, in order to achieve the Sprint Goal. The Product Owner will have a clear idea of which items need to be delivered, but this must be filtered by the Developers' estimation of how many of these items can be delivered within the Sprint.

- How will the work needed to deliver the Increment be achieved? This is accomplished by the Developers creating a plan on how they will deliver the selected items. They represent this plan as a number of tasks. These tasks could involve coding, infrastructure, research, or some other work that contributes toward delivering a backlog item.

The *inputs* for the Sprint Planning are as follows:

- The **Product Backlog**. This is an ordered list of everything that is needed in order to create the product. We'll be talking more about the Product Backlog in *Chapter 5, Scrum Artifacts*.
- The latest Product Increment, which is the cumulative work the team has produced so far.
- Projected developer capacity for the Sprint.

The *outputs* of the Sprint Planning are as follows:

- The Sprint Goal for the upcoming sprint, as discussed earlier in this chapter.
- A list of Product Backlog items that can be Done by the Developers within the Sprint, along with any planned tasks needed to get these items Done. We call this list the **Sprint Backlog**.

So, now that we know the objectives, duration, inputs, and outputs of the Sprint Planning event, let's see what the roles of the Scrum Team members during this event are.

Sprint Planning for the Scrum Master

The Scrum Master ensures that the event takes place and that attendants understand its purpose. The Scrum Master also ensures that the event is kept within its time-box (maximum duration). The Scrum Master may also ask the Developers for clarification on how they intend to achieve the Sprint Goal or create the Sprint's anticipated Increment.

Sprint Planning for the Product Owner

The Product Owner performs two main functions during the Sprint Planning. The first one is that they help set the Sprint Goal. The Sprint Goal will be set in accordance with the product roadmap, current market needs, and the previous Scrum Increment, that is the product functionality that has already been delivered. Although the Product Owner may have the best view on what the best Sprint Goal is, consensus should be reached by the whole of the Scrum Team. The second one is that they help to clarify selected Product Backlog items for the Sprint Backlog and make trade-offs between items when needed. The Product Owner may also ask the Developers for clarification on how they intend to achieve the Sprint Goal or create the Sprint's anticipated Increment.

Sprint Planning for the Developers

The Developers help the Product Owner set a Sprint Goal for the upcoming Sprint. Although the Product Owner should know what the Sprint Goal ought to be, sometimes there may be technical or resource-related reasons that render that goal risky or even unfeasible. This is why the Developers' input in setting the Sprint Goal is invaluable. Once the Sprint Goal is set, the Developers select a number of items from the Product Backlog and add them to the Sprint Backlog. Their selection is influenced by a number of factors:

- Whether an item is contributing toward accomplishing the Sprint Goal.

- **Developer capacity**. This is the Developers' estimated or measured units of work that can be delivered within a Sprint. We'll be exploring this in much more detail in *Chapter 6, Planning and Estimating with Scrum.*

- **The Product Increment**. Previously delivered functionality may affect the estimated cost of an item, as well as its relevance to the Sprint Goal.

> **Important note**
> The number of items selected from the Product Backlog for the Sprint is solely up to the Developers. The Product Owner may suggest certain items, but only the Developers may decide what they will deliver in the upcoming Sprint.

Having set the Sprint Goal and selected the Product Backlog items for the Sprint, the Developers will then decide how to build this functionality into a Done Product Increment during the Sprint. This will usually involve creating a number of work items or tasks, added to the Sprint Backlog, which will help decompose the work needed to deliver in the selected Product Backlog items. These work items should be scoped to 1 day's effort or less.

> **Tip**
> The team shouldn't try to decompose every single selected Product Backlog item into work items or tasks. They should only try to define work for the first few days of the Sprint. The Sprint Backlog can (and should) be modified during the Sprint, as existing work items require modification or become redundant and new work items become apparent. After all, being Agile requires having an iterative workflow that is adaptable to change.

Once the Sprint Planning is complete, the Developers start working on the selected items. This brings us nicely to our next Scrum Event.

Keeping on the right track with the Daily Scrum

The Daily Scrum is a daily occurring event held at the same time and place every day, usually at the start of the day. The Daily Scrum is solely for the benefit of the Developers. The Scrum Master and Product Owner may attend the event, but only as observers. They are not allowed to disrupt or participate. The Scrum Master may want to be present to ensure the meeting does not exceed its maximum duration (time-box) of 15 minutes and that it is not disrupted by external people.

The objective of the event is for the Developers to inspect the work done since the last Daily Scrum and plan the work for the next 24 hours. The structure of the event and the way it's conducted is entirely up to the Developers. A common structure is that each team member gives a brief summary on three things:

- What they've been working on since the last Daily Scrum

- What they plan to work on in the next 24 hours

- Any potential impediments they may be having

It is also common for the event to be conducted in the presence of a Sprint board (more on these in *Chapter 7, The Scrum Journey*). This helps visually display current work progress and the remaining work.

The provides a daily opportunity to inspect and adapt. It means that extra or redundant work may be identified sooner, rather than later, and the Sprint Backlog can be modified accordingly. The Developers often meet immediately after the Daily Scrum for discussions on how to adapt, or to re-plan, the rest of the Sprint's work. It also means that any obstacles to completing the work (impediments) can be dealt with and resolved as early as possible. The Daily Scrum facilitates quick decision-making and frequent communication and collaboration, in accordance with Scrum and Agile principles.

The Daily Scrum allows us to inspect our daily work during the Sprint. At the end of the Sprint, however, we get a chance to inspect our overall Sprint work. Let's see how this is done.

Inspecting the product during the Sprint Review

The Sprint Review is held at the end of the Sprint in order to inspect the Product Increment and adapt the Product Backlog, if needed. The event's duration is at most 4 hours for 1-month Sprints and proportionately shorter for shorter Sprints. The event is attended by the whole of the Scrum Team, but also any stakeholders invited at the Product Owner's discretion.

The *inputs* of the event are the Product Backlog and the done Product Increment produced in the Sprint. The *output* of the event is a revised Product Backlog that identifies the probable Product Backlog items for the next Sprint. The Product Backlog may also be adjusted overall to meet new business opportunities.

The purpose of the Sprint Review is to inspect the Increment, communicate and share knowledge within the Scrum Team but also with any present stakeholders, and adapt the product roadmap, if necessary. The roles of the Scrum Team members during this event are as follows:

- The Product Owner explains what Product Backlog items have been Done and what hasn't been Done. They invite feedback from the stakeholders, and they review the current position of the product in the marketplace, timescales, budget, future capabilities, and the next anticipated releases of functionality or capability of the product.

  They also discuss the state of the Product Backlog and they project likely target and delivery dates based on current metrics (if needed). They also track the total work remaining to reach certain milestones or releases.

- The Developers discuss what went well during the Sprint, what work had to be added, and what had to be removed. They also bring up any problems they encountered and talk about how those problems were solved. Finally, the team demonstrates the work they did for the Increment, receives feedback on it, and answers questions about it.

- The Scrum Master ensures that the event takes place and does not exceed its maximum duration and that the attendees understand its purpose.

By the end of the Sprint Review, both the Scrum Team and the stakeholders should have a clear view of what to do next. In this sense, the Sprint Review also provides valuable input for the next Sprint Planning.

While Sprint Planning allows us to inspect the product, a healthy team should also take time to inspect itself and its work practices. The next event allows us to do just that.

Inspecting the team with the Sprint Retrospective

The Sprint Retrospective is the last event to take place during the Sprint and signifies the end of the Sprint. It is an opportunity for the Scrum Team to inspect itself and create a plan for improvements to be enacted during the next Sprint. It is time-boxed at a maximum of 3 hours for a 1-month Sprint, and proportionately shorter for shorter Sprints. The event is attended by the entire Scrum Team.

The purpose of the Sprint Retrospective is for the Scrum Team to do the following:

- Inspect how it performed with regard to interpersonal relationships, processes, and tools.

- Identify and order the things that went well and the things that didn't.

- Create a plan for implementing improvements to the way it works.

Some of the basic questions the team is called to answer during the Sprint Retrospective are as follows:

- What went well during the Sprint?

- What didn't go well during the Sprint?

- What improvements can we make for the next Sprint?

There are different techniques for eliciting answers to these questions. One of the most effective, yet simple, ones is to just ask each Scrum Team member to create a list of things covering the following relating to the team:

- Start doing.

- Stop doing.

- Continue doing.

The items in this list will often be work-related, such as using specific processes, designs, or tools, for instance. Sometimes they may be related to the environment or infrastructure, for example, a team member may need a faster computer, or they may find the office too noisy for them to focus on their work. Some other times there may be inter personal or recreational ideas, such as setting up weekly knowledge-sharing presentations, for instance. Anything that either helps or prevents the team from working as a self-managing team productively should be brought up at this event. It is advisable that the Scrum Team choose at least one high-priority process improvement and add it to the Sprint Backlog for the next Sprint.

> **Important note**
>
> One of the most important items that may come out of a Sprint Retrospective is a modification of the Definition of Done. Sometimes the existing definition may not reflect the quality standards expected by the team, organization, or stakeholders and must be adapted. The Definition of Done should be reviewed frequently at Sprint Retrospectives.

It is up to the Scrum Team to decide on the best way to organize and structure the Sprint Retrospective. As usual, the Scrum Master should provide coaching and guidance on different techniques and methods to conduct this event.

Summary

In this chapter, we learned what the Scrum Events are, when they take place, how long they last, who attends them, and what their purpose is. We understood how to prepare for the Sprint and how to plan for it in the Sprint Planning. We saw how the Daily Scrum helps us focus on completing the work we committed to in the Sprint. We realized how the Sprint Review and the Sprint Retrospective provide opportunities to learn, adapt, and improve our product, process, and team.

The Scrum Events provide practical and regular support for the pillars of Scrum (transparency, inspection, and adaptation). As such, they must be observed and understood by the Scrum Team. Skipping out on or omitting events undermines the foundations of the Scrum framework. It is the job of the Scrum Master to ensure this doesn't happen.

The Scrum Events will be even better understood when we put them in the context of the Scrum Artifacts, which we will do in the following chapter, so stay tuned for that!

Questions

1. The Developers should not be interrupted during the Sprint. The Sprint Goal should remain intact. These are conditions that foster creativity, quality, and productivity. Which one of the following statements is false?

    a) The Product Owner can help clarify or optimize the Sprint when asked by the Developers.

    b) The Developers may work with the Product Owner to remove or add work from the Sprint Backlog if they find they have more or less capacity than anticipated.

    c) The Sprint Backlog is fully formulated in the Sprint Planning meeting and does not change during the Sprint.

    d) As selected Product Backlog items are decomposed and analyzed further, the Sprint Backlog may change and grow as new work emerges.

2. What does it mean to say that an event is time-boxed? (Choose the best answer)

    a) The event can take no more than a maximum amount of time.

    b) The event must happen by a given time.

    c) The event must take at least a minimum amount of time.

    d) The event must happen at a set time.

3. The time-box for the Sprint Planning meeting is what? (Choose the best answer)

    a) Monthly.

    b) Every 2 weeks.

    c) 8 hours for a monthly Sprint. For shorter Sprints, it is usually shorter.

    d) Between 4 and 8 hours.

4. What is the most accurate description of the purpose of the Daily Scrum for the Developers? (Choose one)

    a) To make changes to the Sprint Backlog

    b) To inform the Scrum Master of work progress

    c) To inspect work done since the last Daily Scrum and plan work to be done in the next 24 hours

    d) To inspect work done since the start of the Sprint and plan work to be done until the end of the Sprint

5. The maximum duration of the Sprint Review (its time-box) is what? (Choose one)

    a) 1 day.

    b) 2 hours.

    c) As long as needed.

    d) At least 4 hours, longer if needed.

    e) 4 hours for a monthly Sprint. For shorter Sprints, it is usually shorter.

6. True or false: The Scrum Team should choose at least one high-priority process improvement, identified during the Sprint Retrospective, and place it in the Product Backlog:

    a) True

    b) False

7. When should the Definition of Done be changed?

    a) Before every Sprint

    b) When it does not reflect the quality standards expected by the team, organization, or stakeholders

    c) Never

    d) During the Daily Scrum

Further reading

- *The Scrum Guide, Ken Schwaber and Jeff Sutherland,* `https://www.scrumguides.org/docs/scrumguide/v2017/2017-Scrum-Guide-US.pdf`

- *Essential Scrum: A Practical Guide to the Most Popular Agile Process, Kenneth S. Rubin, Addison-Wesley, July 2012*

- *Scrum Field Guide, The: Agile Advice for Your First Year and Beyond, Mike Cohn, Addison-Wesley, December 2015*

- *BDD Confusion: Using Behaviour Driven Development for Acceptance Criteria, Chris Lewis, Carnsa Development Series, October 2019*

5
Scrum Artifacts

We looked at how the Scrum Team regularly attends Scrum Events in *Chapter 4, Scrum Events*, as part of a constant inspection and adaptation cycle. These Scrum Events involve creating, reviewing, and modifying certain artifacts; namely, the **Product Backlog**, the **Sprint Backlog**, and the **Product Increment**.

In this chapter, we are going to examine these artifacts in greater detail. We will learn how to add value to the development process by undertaking certain commitments through artifact creation. We will learn how to capture requirements in the Product Backlog as user stories by using the three Cs and INVEST, as well as features, using impact mapping. Additionally, we will find out how to refine the Product Backlog, create a Sprint Backlog, and create a Definition of Done.

We will cover the following topics in this chapter:

- Understanding the value of Scrum Artifacts
- Creating and managing the Product Backlog
- Creating and managing the Sprint Backlog
- Producing an Increment

Let's start by learning how Scrum Artifacts add value to our product development.

Understanding the value of Scrum Artifacts

Scrum Artifacts enable frequent inspections by the Scrum Team and the stakeholders and allow us to detect undesirable deviations from the road toward product delivery. They represent work that's performed to provide transparency and opportunities for inspection and adaptation (see *The pillars of empiricism section in Chapter 2, Scrum Theory and Principles*). The work each artifact represents is as follows:

- The **Product Backlog** captures an ordered list of the project requirements and allows us to create a product roadmap and define the items to tackle in a sprint.

- The **Sprint Backlog** enables us to clearly identify the work we intend to produce during a Sprint, set alongside a Sprint Goal (see *Chapter 4, Scrum Events*, the *Starting the Sprint with Sprint Planning* section).

- The **Product Increment** allows us to inspect the functionality of the work we produced and potentially expose it to the stakeholders.

The artifacts and the relationships between them are depicted in the following diagram:

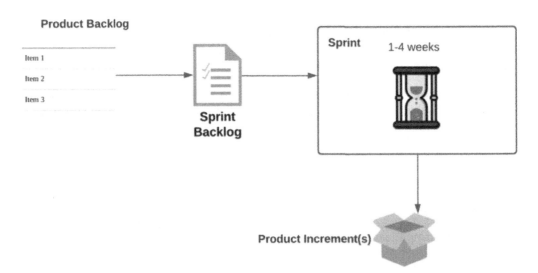

Figure 5.1 – Scrum Artifacts

The Product Backlog is used to produce the Sprint Backlog. Developers work on Sprint Backlog items through the Sprint, and they deliver them as a Product Increment.

Put together, these three artifacts represent a holistic view of the software development lifecycle, from requirements (Product Backlog) to planning and development (Sprint Backlog) to usable software (Product Increment).

Each artifact contains a *commitment* to ensure it provides information that enhances transparency and focuses on how progress can be measured:

- For the Product Backlog, the commitment is the **Product Goal**.
- For the Sprint Backlog, the commitment is the **Sprint Goal**.
- For the Increment, the commitment is the **Definition of Done**.

These commitments exist to reinforce empiricism and the Scrum values for the Scrum Team and their stakeholders.

It's also important to realize that the artifacts we'll be examining in this chapter are not the only ones that will – or should – be produced during Scrum. Scrum Teams may also produce a variety of other artifacts to help improve inspection and adaptation, such as burn-up or burn-down charts (more on these in *Chapter 6, Planning and Estimating with Scrum in the Burn-Up and Burn-Down Charts section*), Test Plans, and others. However, the Product Backlog, Sprint Backlog, and Product Increment are the only artifacts *mandated by Scrum*, and they form the core of any Scrum Team planning and decision-making activities. Let's explore the first artifact we'll need to create in order to start our Scrum journey.

Creating and managing the Product Backlog

The Product Backlog is an ordered list of everything that is needed in the product. Each product has its own unique backlog. It is the *only* source of planned work for the product. The Product Backlog is a living artifact; it is constantly in flux as requirements and market conditions change. The following diagram provides an overview of the role and significance of the Product Backlog:

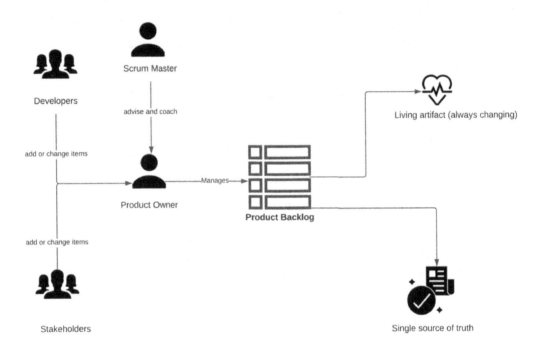

Figure 5.2 – Product Backlog items as user stories

As shown in the preceding diagram, the Product Owner is the only role with direct access to the Product Backlog. The Scrum Guide states that the Product Owner is responsible for managing the Product Backlog. This can be interpreted in many ways, but it does imply that the Product Owner has the final say on the Product Backlog. Therefore, it is advisable that developers or stakeholders who wish to add or change items on the Product Backlog do so under the guidance and approval of the Product Owner. Without interfering or confusing changes, the Product Backlog is the single source of truth for the product's requirements and planned work. This means that the developers create work based on Product Backlog items and nothing else. The Product Owner is responsible for the backlog's content, availability, and ordering. The Scrum Master serves the Product Owner by suggesting techniques for defining the Product Goal and managing the backlog.

Making a commitment – the Product Goal

Items are inserted into the Product Backlog to fulfill the **Product Goal**. The Product Goal describes the future state of the product, which can serve as a target for the Scrum Team to focus on and plan against. The Product Owner is responsible for defining and explicitly communicating the Product Goal. The Product Goal is a long-term objective for the Scrum Team. Every product decision should be taken with a view of accomplishing this objective.

There are many ways to write the Product Goal, but for it to be really useful, we should take the following into consideration:

- What are we doing? In other words, what are the characteristics of our product? Who are we doing it for? Who's going to benefit the most from our product?

- How are they benefiting? What is our product's **unique selling point** (USP)? What do we offer over our competitors?

The electric vehicle manufacturer Tesla set this product goal for their Model S car:

A four-door sedan that seats seven people (up to five adults and two kids) can go 300 miles on a single charge and 0-60 mph in under 4.5 seconds.

Here, they clearly set out the characteristics of their product (a four-door, seven-seater sedan) and who's going to benefit most from it (families with kids) and the USPs (long range, great acceleration). This is a concise and informative Product Goal that served as the basis for the delivery of a great product.

As with everything in Scrum, a Product Goal is subject to inspection and adaptation. As market conditions change, so should our Product Goal. Organizations where the Product Goal remains unaltered for months or years on end are usually oblivious to external changes and influences. The Product Goal helps us determine which items to add to our Product Backlog. The following section explains how this happens.

Creating Backlog items as user stories

The Scrum Guide refers to the Product Backlog as a generic list of items. It does not specify what these items should be other than that they should have the attributes of a description, order, estimate, and value. The de facto standard for representing such items is the **user story**. Not everyone can quite agree on an exact definition of a user story, but the following is a widely accepted one:

A user story is a concise description of some required functionality told from the perspective of the person who needs or desires it.

User stories may be written in many formats, but the most commonly used template is as follows:

As a <type of user>, I want <some goal> so that <I receive some benefit>.

Some examples of user stories are as follows:

- As a vegetarian pizza buyer, I want to see only the vegetarian toppings so that I can order a pizza without getting distracted by toppings I won't choose.

- As a bank account holder, I want to see how much interest I earned in the last year, so that I can decide whether to keep or change my account.

- As the marketing manager, I need to see what geographical locations our system logins are from, so that I can understand our clients' demographics better.

- As a displeased customer, I want to quickly, and easily, describe my issues to the business so that I can have them rectified.

A typical Product Backlog will look as follows:

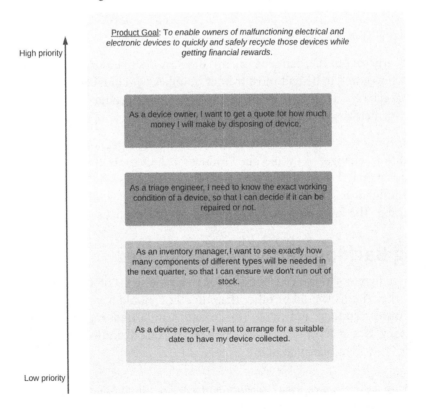

Figure 5.3 – Product Backlog items as user stories

As we can see, the backlog is a list of ordered user stories and a Product Goal. User stories are meant to serve as the start of a conversation about the enclosing requirements. They are an implicit contract between the Product Owner and the developers. The developers commit to talking to the Product Owner about the story before working on it. The Product Owner commits to being available to the developers to answer questions about the story, whenever that may be. This implicit contract is essential in an Agile environment as it allows work on requirements to begin, even though all the details may not be known.

The vast majority of requirements start out as thinly sketched user stories that ultimately get fleshed out with details. One of the problems with user stories is that they can be used to describe some broad and generic requirements. This can make it difficult to analyze and prioritize them. Fortunately, there are some techniques that can help us with that. Let's take a quick look at them.

Creating Stories with the three Cs

The three Cs denote the three critical aspects of a user story:

- **Card**: The **card** here refers to the index card or post-it note that was originally used to capture user stories. The point here is that the story should capture the essence of the requirements and not a full specification of the intended functionality. Notes such as priority, size estimate ,and acceptance criteria may also be part of the story. The rest should be derived through conversation with the Product Owner.

- **Conversation**: This is where the details of the requirements and derived functional behaviors are brought to light. Conversations are between the developers and the Product Owner (or stakeholders that have been referred to by the Product Owner). These conversations usually take place several times as the mutual understanding about the requirements increases. Documentation may also be generated because of these conversations, such as BDD feature files, for instance.

- **Confirmation**: We need to be able to verify whether our work actually produces the value the user story encapsulates. The best way to do that is to identify some acceptance criteria; that is, conditions that indicate when the story has delivered the required value to the stakeholders.

Keeping the three Cs in mind when creating user stories will go a long way toward creating precise and unambiguous user stories that can easily be implemented by developers.

INVESTing in high-quality user stories

INVEST is an acronym that stands for a set of criteria that a good user story should adhere to. It provides a useful mnemonic of six basic quality principles that should apply to a story. Let's examine them:

- **Independent**: No user story should rely on another one. We should be able to prioritize any story in the backlog individually, without triggering a cascade of dependent stories.

- **Negotiable**: Stories are not specifications. A story should always leave room for discussion. A good story will capture the essence of the requirements, but details must be derived by having conversations.

- **Valuable**: Stories must deliver value to stakeholders. Stories that capture *fun*, *hobby*, or *gold-plating* (unnecessary future improvements) requirements should not be added to the Product Backlog.

- **Estimable**: Stories must contain enough information as to make it possible to estimate the relative size or complexity of them. This means that the developers must be able to have a fair idea of what needs to be done, after reading the story.

- **Small**: Stories should be scoped and sized in such a way that they can be implemented within a Sprint.

- **Testable**: There should be a way to test a user story, even though the exact way to do so may not be obvious or possible yet. The best way to achieve this is to add measurable and objective acceptance criteria to the story.

The INVEST guidelines ensure that we can write stories at the right level of detail and scope them correctly.

Adhering to the 3Cs and INVEST principles is essential in avoiding a common side effect of user story-based Product Backlogs: *story card hell*. This occurs when the backlog consists of numerous user stories that are so widely scoped and lacking in context that the backlog becomes extremely difficult to prioritize, classify, and estimate. Another way to avoid this situation is to capture requirements as impact maps and create a feature-based Product Backlog.

Creating Product Backlog items as features

This approach ensures that vague requirements, including user stories, are never added to the Product Backlog. This is achieved by analyzing the requirements and modeling them as impact maps. Impact mapping allows us to identify and define features that are specific and well-scoped items of functionality that help implement the capabilities stakeholders require from our product. An impact map template is shown in the following diagram:

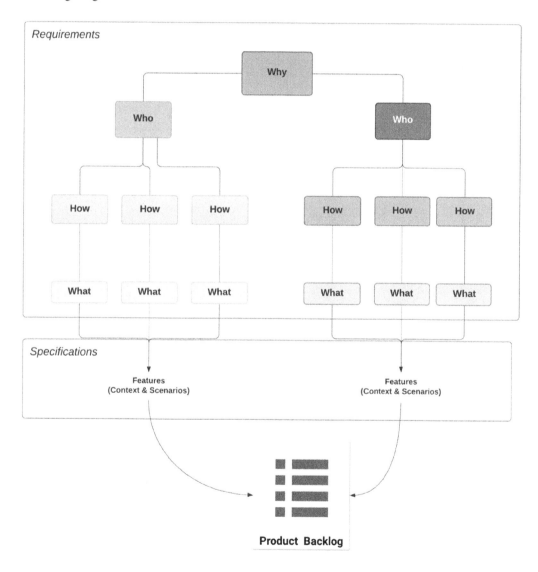

Figure 5.4 – Requirements as an impact map

An impact map provides us with a structured, hierarchical view of our requirements. It gives a clear visualization of the stakeholders, their goals, and the broader capabilities they require of our product to accomplish those goals.

The identified features provide the content of our Product Backlog. They are presented in the context of their respective capabilities, as shown in the following diagram:

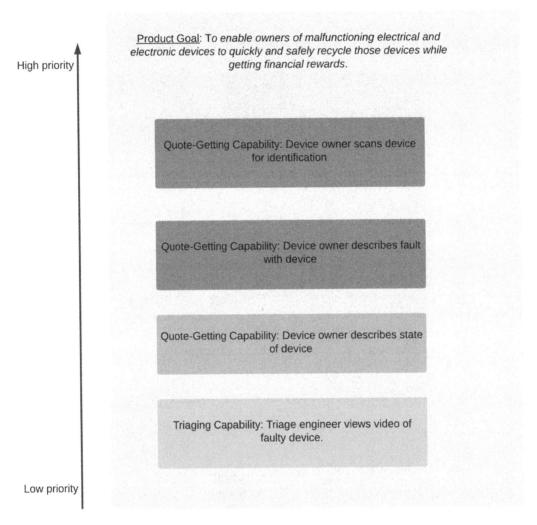

Figure 5.5 – Product Backlog items as features

As we can see, this Product Backlog's content consists of specific, well-scoped, and contextualized features. Features are associated with broader capabilities, which, in turn, are associated with stakeholders and their goals. This is the basis of a feature-first approach, as detailed in my other book, *Managing Software Requirements the Agile Way*.

Regardless of how we choose to represent these items in the Product Backlog, one thing is certain: we always start out by defining high-level, coarse-grained items, which we then proceed to refine and analyze in a process known as Product Backlog refinement. Let's take a closer look at this.

Refining the Product Backlog

Product Backlog refinement is the act of breaking down and further defining Product Backlog items into smaller, more precise items. This is an ongoing activity that adds item details, such as a detailed description, order, and size or complexity estimates. Refinement helps us add value to the product by correctly identifying and scoping backlog items. It helps us deal with changes and makes it easier to plan for the next Sprint.

The Product Owner is responsible for refining the Product Backlog but does not usually perform this on their own. The Product Owner must work with the developers to communicate and clarify item details, obtain estimates, and identify technical risks with backlog items. The Scrum Master may also help the Product Owner find techniques for effective item definition and methods for prioritizing and classifying items.

There is no prescribed time frame for how much time should be spent refining the backlog. My experience suggests that 10% of the Sprint's length usually provides adequate time for refinement in most cases. I would also strongly advise that dedicated time is set apart each Sprint for backlog refinement with the participation of the whole Scrum Team. This should be done preferably in multiple meetings based on the Sprint's length. For example, in a 2-week sprint (10 working days), I would try to set apart two half-day sessions, one each week, for backlog refinement. This time should be taken into account when the developers create the Sprint Backlog (see the *Creating and managing the Sprint Backlog* section) and when they estimate their work capacity for the Sprint.

Now that we have discussed how to create and manage the Product Backlog, let's examine how to do the same for its temporary subset, the Sprint Backlog.

Creating and managing the Sprint Backlog

The Sprint Backlog is simply a list of Product Backlog items that have been selected for the Sprint, along with the plan for delivering them and accomplishing the **Sprint Goal**. While the Product Owner is responsible for which items go in the Product Backlog, the developers are solely accountable for which items go into the Sprint Backlog. The Product Owner will make suggestions as to which items should go in the Sprint Backlog, but the developers will decide based on their estimation of the work needed for each item and their own capacity to deliver work within the Sprint. Often, if the Product Owner is very insistent on including certain items in the Sprint, the developers may exclude other items of equal size or complexity from the Sprint Backlog so that they can accommodate the high-priority item. Placing and removing items from the Sprint Backlog must always be driven by the Sprint Goal's imperative. Let's discuss how that happens.

Making a commitment – the Sprint Goal

The artifact commitment for the Sprint Backlog is the Sprint Goal. This aims to capture the reason this Sprint is undertaken. It encapsulates the objective of the Sprint. Progress toward the Sprint Goal is inspected daily, during the Daily Scrum (see *Keeping on the right track with the Daily Scrum* section in *Chapter 4, Scrum Events*). If needed, developers may adapt the Sprint Backlog as necessary by adjusting the upcoming planned work. As the developers work during the Sprint, they keep the Sprint Goal in mind. If the work turns out to be different than anticipated, they communicate with the Product Owner to adjust the scope of the Sprint Backlog within the Sprint, without affecting the Sprint Goal.

A Sprint Goal must be unambiguous and achievable within the Sprint. The Scrum Master must ensure the Sprint Goal is transparent and visible to all stakeholders and that the Scrum Team agrees on when the Sprint Goal has been achieved; that is, to establish certain criteria to help assess the Sprint Goal's completeness.

Let's look at an example. A Sprint Goal that states, for example, *Improve website performance* is simply too vague to be useful. A good Sprint Goal would say *Decrease the page load times for listings and payments*. The team would have to agree on the criteria for determining the success of the Sprint Goal, such as *A full product listing must be shown within 2 seconds* or *The payment page must load twice as fast as in the previous increment*.

As another example, let's look at the *Facilitate user on-boarding* Sprint Goal. We could have already identified two user stories (or features) for user onboarding, such as *allow the user to log in with their Twitter credentials* and *Create an interactive tutorial for our app*. We need to clarify which of these methods we'll be implementing to achieve our Sprint Goal; otherwise, it will be difficult to judge whether we achieved it or not. It could well be that we decide to implement both features within the Sprint. That is fine, but we then need to change our Sprint Goal to *Facilitate user onboarding with a Twitter login and interactive tutorial*.

Clear and measurable Sprint Goals help the team focus and interact on what really adds value to our product during a Sprint. They also make it much easier to plan for the Sprint. Let's examine what we mean by Sprint planning.

Planning for the Sprint

The plan for delivering the work needed to deliver the Sprint Backlog items consists of the Product Backlog items selected for the Sprint, as well as the tasks required to implement those items. If an item is *what we need to deliver*, the plan is *what we need to do in order to deliver it*. For instance, if the work item is something such as *As a gadget owner I want to describe the fault with the gadget so that I can get an estimate for recycling it*, then the plan may involve creating the following tasks:

- Create a database schema for the gadget's description
- Create a HTML form for the gadget's description
- Add a web app endpoint for the gadget's description
- Integrate the gadget database into the **Show Gadgets** page

There are probably many others too.

> **Important note**
>
> Sprint Backlog items are never *owned* by a single developer. The developers, as a team, assume collective ownership of the Sprint Backlog items and are responsible for accomplishing the Sprint Goal. Even though an individual developer may be working exclusively on an item, the developers are collectively responsible for the item's successful delivery.

As with all Scrum Artifacts, the Sprint Backlog should be highly visible and transparent to all stakeholders. The output of the Sprint Backlog is a Product Increment of working software, which leads us conveniently to the following section.

Producing a Product Increment

A **Product Increment** is the working software that's created during the Sprint. It is a demonstrable stepping stone toward the Product Goal. Each increment is cumulative to previous increments and thoroughly verified, ensuring that all the Increments work together. An Increment must do the following:

- Be usable – a usable increment is a piece of software that can be used by stakeholders to enact some functionality required and related to the Sprint Goal.

- Meet the Definition of Done, as discussed in the *Making a commitment – Definition of Done* section.

An Increment is created the moment a Sprint Backlog item meets the Definition of Done.

> **Important note**
> Multiple Increments may be created within a Sprint. The sum of all Sprint Increments is presented at the Sprint Review so that all the work can be inspected. However, an Increment may be delivered to stakeholders before the end of the Sprint. Value, in the shape of working code, can be released anytime during a Sprint, not just at the Sprint Review.

As discussed in *Chapter 4, Scrum Events*, Increments must be deliverable, but they don't always have to be delivered at each Sprint. The Product Owner will decide if it makes sense for an Increment to be delivered to the stakeholders.

The Scrum Master may help the Scrum Team focus on creating high-value Increments that meet the Definition of Done. Let's see what **Done** really means.

Making a commitment – Definition of Done

Many developers throughout the ages have asked the same question: When is a piece of software done? The answer is usually subjective. For some people, *done* means that the software does what they want it to do. For others, it's when it does what their clients want it to do. For many, software is done only when fully tested. For others, it is done when it has been successfully deployed to a server or to the internet. That is why having a shared Definition of Done is so important.

The **Definition of Done** ensures that everyone understands when the work for an item that's being implemented as part of the Increment is complete. It also means that the work is *potentially shippable;* that is, it can be deployed and delivered to the stakeholders for review. If a Product Backlog item does not meet the Definition of Done, it cannot be released or even presented at the Sprint Review.

Many Agile organizations have a common Definition of Done that they apply to all their product development. In this case, different Scrum Teams will use that definition as their baseline, but they may also add their own criteria and regress points to extend the definition. If such a definition does not exist, it is up to the Scrum Team to come up with one that is most suitable to them.

What we define as Done depends mainly on the product we're delivering, the domain we're working in, and the organizational culture. The Definition of Done may encompass many different criteria. Usually, these are a combination (of many or all) of the following:

- Unit tests are passing, ensuring the Increment is coded correctly.

- Functional tests are passing, ensuring the increment functions correctly.

- Integration tests are passing, ensuring the increment works well within the wider context of our system or network.

- Continuous Integration build is passing, ensuring the increment works on a staging or deployment environment.

- Code has been peer-reviewed, ensuring that best practices are being followed and design or coding flaws have been picked up.

- Documentation has been created, ensuring everyone understands how and why the increment works.

- The Increment has been user tested, ensuring the end users are satisfied with the software.

Naturally, this isn't a conclusive list; these are just some of the most common criteria for defining Done.

> **Important note**
> The definition of Done is an absolute. Work is either done or it isn't. There can be no *but it meets three of the four criteria for done* arguments. If an item cannot be classed as Done, then it must be placed back in the Product Backlog for further consideration.

The Definition of Done may be revised during the Sprint Retrospective event (*Chapter 4, Scrum Events, in the Starting the Sprint with Sprint Planning* Section). For instance, after several Sprints, you may discover that the current definition is not fit for purpose and needs to be adapted. This is not uncommon and is perfectly in line with the Scrum pillars of continuous transparency, inspection, and adaptation. It helps the Scrum Team focus on creating high-value, high-quality Increments.

Summary

In this chapter, we looked at Scrum Artifacts. We learned why we create those artifacts and the commitments we make when creating them. We saw how to create a Product Backlog and a Product Goal, how to select Product Backlog items for our Sprint Backlog, and how to define a Sprint Goal. We discussed Product Increments and learned how to define Done. We also examined when the artifacts are created, how they can be modified, and who's accountable for them.

Scrum Artifacts are designed to maximize the transparency of key information. They are key decision-making tools in the product development process. Therefore, it is very important that we know the artifacts' roles within Scrum and understand the value they add.

This chapter brings us to the end of the first section of this book, which covered the fundamentals of the Scrum framework. In the second section, we'll look at all the other things we need to do to make Scrum work in the real world – things that are not covered by the Scrum Guide. We'll start this with *Chapter 6, Planning and Estimating with Scrum*. Keep reading because this is where Scrum gets really interesting!

Questions

1. The CEO asks the developers to add a *very important* item to a Sprint that is in progress. What should the developers do? (Choose the best answer.)

    a) Add the item to the Sprint Backlog immediately.

    b) Add the item to the Sprint Backlog, but only if the item is in line with the Sprint Goal.

    c) Add the item to the Sprint Backlog and drop an item of equal size.

    d) Inform the Product Owner so that they can work with the CEO.

2. True or False: When multiple teams work together on the same product, each team should maintain a separate Product Backlog.

    a) True.

    b) False.

3. Which of the following provides the Scrum Team with an objective and overarching direction for the Sprint? (Choose one.)

    a) The Sprint Backlog

    b) The Sprint Goal

    c) The Product Goal

    d) The Definition of Done

4. Halfway through the Sprint, the developers have already produced an Increment that is usable and *Done*. The stakeholders are very interested in reviewing the Increment as soon as possible. What should the Scrum Team do?

    a) Release the Increment to the Stakeholders as soon as possible.

    b) Tell the Stakeholders that the sum of all Increments will be delivered at the Sprint Review.

    c) Tell the Stakeholders that the sum of all Increments will be delivered at the end of the Sprint.

    d) Tell the Stakeholders that the Increment will be delivered at the end of the Sprint.

5. When does a developer take ownership of a Sprint Backlog item?

    a) During the Sprint Planning Event.

    b) When the developer is free to start working on an item.

    c) When the most senior developer says so.

    d) Never. The developers assume collective ownership of all and any items, even if a single developer is working on them alone.

6. True or False: The purpose of a Sprint is to produce a done Increment of a product.

   a) True.

   b) False.

7. Who creates the *Definition of Done*? (Choose one answer.)

   a) The Scrum Master, as they are meant to advise the Scrum Team on the best practices.

   b) The organization (or the Scrum Team, if there is no organizational definition).

   c) The Product Owner, since they are responsible for the product's success.

   d) The developers under the guidance of the Scrum Master.

8. When must the Product Owner release an Increment to the stakeholders? (Choose one.)

   a) Always

   b) After the Sprint Review

   c) When it makes sense to do so

   d) When the Scrum Master approves it

9. When should Product Backlog refinement take place? (Choose one.)

   a) Continuously during the Sprint

   b) After the Sprint Review

   c) At the start of the Sprint

   d) At the end of the Sprint

Further reading

- *The Scrum Guide, Ken Schwaber and Jeff Sutherland* (`https://www.scrumguides.org/docs/scrumguide/v2017/2017-Scrum-Guide-US.pdf`)

- *User Stories Applied: For Agile Software Development, Mike Cohn, Addison-Wesley, 2004*

- *Managing Software Requirements the Agile Way, Fred Heath, Packt Publishing, 2020*

Section 2: Scrum in Action

In this part, you will learn how to go beyond the authentic Scrum framework, best practices and patterns when using Scrum, and how to prepare for the PSM I exam.

This section comprises the following chapters:

- *Chapter 6, Planning and Estimating with Scrum*
- *Chapter 7, The Sprint Journey*
- *Chapter 8, Facets of Scrum*

6
Planning and Estimating with Scrum

In the previous chapters, we examined the fundamental concepts and components of Scrum and obtained precious knowledge about them. Although this knowledge is essential, it is *not enough to successfully deliver a software project*. This is not a weakness on Scrum's part. It is simply that, as we have mentioned in previous chapters, Scrum *is a framework, not a process or methodology*. Scrum sets rules, responsibilities, and guidelines about how to develop software but doesn't dictate which methods or techniques to use.

Scrum Teams use different methodologies and processes for software development, and some of them have become de facto standards in Scrum. In this chapter, we will examine two fundamental concepts about software project management and how we can implement them in a Scrum-compatible manner. These concepts are **estimating** and **planning**. These are inextricably linked to one another; you can't plan without estimating, and there's no point in estimating unless you intend to have a plan. Being able to estimate and plan accurately enables us to forecast – that is, project – our estimates into the future.

So, in this chapter, we will learn how to create a product roadmap, estimate backlog items, and use our estimates to determine our team's velocity. We will then use that knowledge to help us track and forecast our progress with burnup/down charts.

The topics we will cover in this chapter are as follows:

- Managing the art of estimation
- Planning with the product roadmap
- Forecasting with velocity and burn charts

Let's start our journey by learning how to estimate.

Managing the art of estimation

Estimation is an essential part of software development and project management. Some people call it a *necessary evil*. I don't know about the *evil* part, but I certainly agree with the *necessary* part. The Scrum Guide doesn't say anything about how to estimate the items in our Product Backlog. However, the industry has adopted some techniques that we will discuss in the following sections. But first, let's examine why estimation is so important. Having estimates allows the Scrum Team to do the following:

- **Prioritize items in the Product Backlog**: This happens as part of the Backlog refinement process, which we talked about in *Chapter 5, Scrum Artifacts*. There are many ways to prioritize the items in the Product Backlog, and effort or size estimates are one way to do so.

- **Choose which items to place in the Sprint Backlog**: This happens during the Sprint planning event, as described in *Chapter 4, Scrum Events*. If we can't estimate these items, we cannot decide which ones we can work on within a Sprint.

- **Forecast our future work**: A forecast is a calculation of the completion of an item, feature, or product. Estimates are often used to formulate forecasts.

- **Promote analysis and share understanding**: Estimates often serve as the basis of discussion about the value of an item, or even help prompt the elicitation of more precise requirements and deeper analysis about the item.

So, estimation is certainly something all Scrum Team members need to be skilled in. Before we proceed any further, let's clarify what we mean by estimation in the Scrum world.

Important Note

In the Scrum world, we prefer not to use dates or workdays in our estimations. Instead, we prefer to define the effort involved in, or the complexity of, the task we are estimating. We call this unit of effort and/or complexity a **story point**.

A story point *does not* represent units of time. Instead, we can think of it as representing time distributions. Let's suppose that a backlog item is estimated at eight (8) story points. This does not mean that the team will take 8 hours, days, or weeks to complete this item. It just means that the item, *on average*, will take more time to deliver than an item with a smaller value. It also means that, *on average*, it will take less time to deliver than an item with a greater point value. The words *on average* are important here. They imply that most of the time (but not always), that item will take longer than items with smaller values and shorter than items with greater values.

With this in mind, let's look at the two main methods of estimation used by Scrum Teams. We'll start by learning how to choose an estimation scale and how to create a baseline.

Choosing an estimation scale

The first thing we must do before we start the estimation process is choose an estimation scale for our story points. The lower end of the scale should represent items that take the least effort or are the least complex. The high end of the scale should represent items that take the most effort or are the most complex. Many Scrum Teams use the Fibonacci series (1, 2, 3, 5, 8, 13, 21, 34, and so on). Others use a T-shirt size scale (S, M, L, XL, and XXL). I have worked with a team that used fruit to denote the complexity of a task (cherries were the simplest ones, while pineapples were the most complex). Some organizations tend to use a modified Fibonacci series (1/2, 1, 2, 3, 5, 8, 13, 20, 40, and 100) as it's more flexible and readable. Whichever scale you decide to use, it's a good idea to include a value for items that the estimator thinks cannot be estimated or completed within a reasonable time, or to an expected quality. The question mark (?) and infinity (∞) symbols are normally used for that purpose. We would normally mark our chosen scale as a deck of cards and allocate a deck to each developer. A typical deck would look something like this:

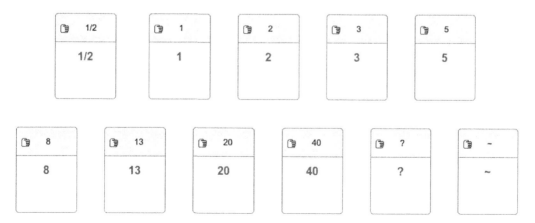

Figure 6.1 – A deck of cards representing estimates

In the deck depicted in the preceding image, the developers would choose the **1/2** card as a point estimate for an item that can be delivered very quickly and easily. They would use the **1** card for an item that's twice as big and complex as the first one, and so on with the rest of the deck.

Developers use such card decks to give estimates during events such as **Sprint planning**. We shall see how this is done in the next few sections.

> **Tip**
> Make sure that all the estimates are processed privately by each developer, without the developers knowing or influencing each other's estimates. This helps us avoid bias and peer pressure when estimating.

Once we've decided on an estimating scale, the next step is to create a baseline. Let's learn how to do that.

Creating a baseline

We mentioned in the preceding section that the smallest-value card in our estimation card deck should represent the item (user story or feature) that requires the least amount of effort and/or has the least complexity. Then, we can estimate the rest of the items in relation to this baseline. The question is, *how do we decide which item that should be*? Some Scrum Teams choose the *easiest* item in their Product Backlog and assign it the lowest estimate value. I don't agree with this approach as it is subjective and temporaneous; it creates a moving baseline that reflects the current items in the backlog instead of a generic and objective representation of effort and complexity. Instead, I suggest that developers think of the simplest item they can think of for the business domain and technologies they are working in.

> **Tip**
> Represent the lowest value in the estimating scale as the simplest item or task that is often used within your team, project, and organization.

In most cases, this would be a `Hello, [username]` type of item, where the system is unconditionally displaying a dynamic message to the user. The message's text could be fetched from a database or an external system call, dependent on what the team feels is representative of their system. Using the estimation scale shown in *Figure 6.1*, such an item would be valued as 1/2 story points. We can then estimate other items relative to this standard and well-known item. The advantage of using an external baseline, such as a `Hello, [username]` item, is that we can apply this to every single Sprint and often across different teams and projects within our organization. It provides an objective and constant baseline.

In addition, I would also suggest having a second baseline value. Choose the median value on your estimation scale, say an 8 on the card deck shown in *Figure 6.1*. Then, think of an item or task that you often encounter that takes a moderate amount of effort to complete or has moderate complexity. So, now, we have two baselines: one for the low-end estimates and one for mid-range estimates. The reason for having two baselines is that it's easier and more accurate to say that an item is two or three times more difficult than another than saying that it's 10 times more difficult. Having two baselines makes it easier to compare items relative to each other.

So, now that we have an estimation scale and a baseline, let's learn how the Scrum Team leverages these to estimate Product Backlog items.

Playing Planning Poker

One of the most popular estimating methods in Scrum is **Planning Poker**. Planning Poker is played by gathering the Scrum Team together and giving each developer a deck of cards with our chosen estimation scale. The process then goes as follows:

1. The Product Owner reads out an item from the Product Backlog, including all the relevant details and contextual information.

2. The developers are called to display a card with their estimate for that item. The display of cards must be simultaneous, and the developers should keep their choice hidden from one another until it's time to display them, in order to avoid bias in the estimation.

3. The developers who had the lowest and highest estimate value will be called to justify their estimates. This will start a discussion between the whole Scrum Team as to the size and complexity of the item.

4. All the developers are then called to give another estimate for the item, considering the previous discussion.

5. *Steps 3* and *4* are repeated until a consensus has been reached as to the estimated value of the item.

6. The Product Owner reads out the next item from the Product Backlog and the process starts again.

A slight variation in the process is that instead of trying to reach consensus through iteration, we can average the estimates to produce a single estimate value. So, we would replace *step 5* with the following:

The median value of the estimates is selected as the estimated value for the item.

This averaging approach is quicker than trying for consensus by repeating displays and is indicated for teams with a larger number of developers. On the flip side, it skips much of a potentially beneficial discussion between the team members. Choose the approach that suits your team's size and composition best.

Tips

If a developer chooses the question mark (?) card as their estimate, they are lacking essential information to make an estimate. The Product Owner should supply the necessary information to allow the estimate to be given. If they are unable to do so, the item should be shelved until there is enough information available.

If developers choose the infinity (∞) card for the estimate, the item is too large or too complex to be worked on as a single item. The team must break the item down into smaller items and estimate these individually.

Estimating backlog items using the bucket method

A different estimating technique is to use estimate *buckets*. These act as locations (usually a paper folder or column on a whiteboard) for each value in our estimation scale (1/2, 1, 2, 3, 5, and so on). The process works as follows:

1. The Product Owner reads out an item from the Product Backlog, including all the relevant details and contextual information. They then hand a card with the item's name (or reference) on it to a developer.

2. The developer places the item card in the *bucket* they feel is suited to that item's estimate.

3. The next developer may leave the item where it is or move it to a different bucket. If they move it to a different bucket, they must justify the move.

    This is repeated until all the developers have had a chance to move the item to a bucket.

4. When the last developer has had their turn, the team is asked whether they are happy with the bucket the item is in. If they aren't, then a discussion between the team ensues until a consensus is reached.

5. The Product Owner reads out the next item from the Product Backlog and hands it to a developer.

This approach is usually quicker in achieving consensus than Planning Poker, but it is susceptible to bias as the developers know of the previous developers' estimates and may be liable to just agree with them instead of *rocking the boat*.

A variation of the *bucket* method is the developers simultaneously placing item cards in buckets. The bucket with the most *hits* is selected as the representative estimate. Once again, individual teams should tailor this method to their own needs.

So, now that we know what estimating is and how to create estimates for our backlog items, we are ready to tackle the other major concept: planning.

Planning ahead with the product roadmap

There is a common misconception about Scrum and Agile methods in general: they don't apply or require any planning. Nothing could be further from the truth. Agile and Scrum both rely on good planning – it's a fundamental part of the Agile philosophy. The main differences between *traditional* planning and Agile planning are as follows:

- Agile planning happens regularly in an iterative and incremental manner.
- Agile planning prefers detailed short-term plans and abstract long-term plans.

We have already learned about the Sprint planning event, which happens at the start of each Sprint. In this section, we will examine how medium- and long-term planning is dealt with in Scrum. To learn about this, we need to understand what drives a Scrum product. So, let's discuss product roadmaps.

Envisioning the product journey with a product roadmap

A product usually begins its lifecycle as an idea or a vision. In Scrum, we express this idea or vision as a **Product Goal**. We already talked about the Product Goal in *Chapter 5, Scrum Artifacts*, and how to create achievable and measurable goals. Scrum Teams use the Product Goal as the context for creating and maintaining the Product Backlog, but many teams also use it as the basis for creating another artifact: the **product roadmap**. This roadmap provides a strategic and actionable plan for realizing the Product Goal. It helps us achieve the following:

- Demonstrate to stakeholders how we are going to realize the Product Goal as a series of activities leading to achievable milestones.

- Clearly identify priorities and initiatives that should be pursued or used to the Product Goal.

- Facilitate the discussion of options and scenario planning.

- Communicate the product strategy to external stakeholders, such as customers.

A product roadmap describes the journey we want our product to go through over the next 12 months or so. It communicates how we envision the product evolving across several releases. There are many ways to create roadmaps. My tips for creating clear and usable product roadmaps are as follows:

- **Maintain a high level of granularity**: Avoid using specific user stories or detailed features in your roadmap. These are fine for short-term, tactical planning, such as the Sprint planning event. The product roadmap, however, is a medium-to-long-term strategic planning tool. Having features or low-level stories in the roadmap will make it difficult to understand and explain, and it also prone to change often. Instead, populate the roadmap with generic, high-level user stories (often called **epics**). If you're using impact mapping, as outlined in *Chapter 5, Scrum Artifacts*, then *capabilities* are great abstractions to place on the roadmap.

- **Avoid using fixed dates**: First, it's impossible to predict an event 6 months into the future with great accuracy. Second, dates are often taken as immutable promises or commitments by the stakeholders, and that seldom ends well. Use time periods instead, such as financial year quarters.

- **Don't look too far into the future**: Uncertainty only increases with time. Most product roadmaps need revising every 6 months or so; therefore, it is pointless having a roadmap that spans over a year.

With that in mind, let's see what a product roadmap looks like:

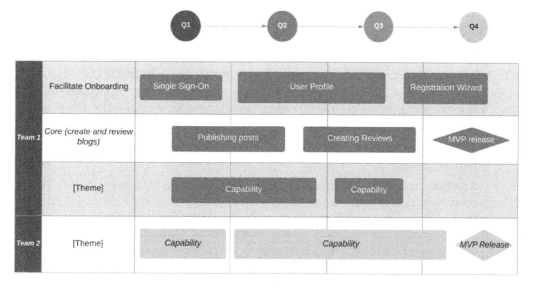

Figure 6.2 – A product roadmap

Let's take a closer look at this roadmap. There are four things we need to note:

- First, it consists of four columns, each for a quarter of the financial year. We could have used calendar months or even weeks, but that would only make the roadmap more elaborate and subject to constant revision.

- The second thing is that we are using swim lanes to indicate the activities of the two teams (**Team 1** and **Team 2**) working on the product. This makes it easy to envisage how work is distributed within the organization and take the budget and resources that have been allocated to each team into account.

- Third, we are using distinct themes, such as **Facilitate Onboarding** and **Core Functionality**, to capture related workstreams or capabilities. This facilitates identifying the associated capabilities needed to complete a certain theme. For instance, the first lane of our roadmap indicates that Team 1 will be working on the **Facilitate Onboarding** theme and planning to deliver the **single sign-on capability** within the first quarter of the year.

- Finally, we are identifying the goals and milestones on our roadmap. In our example, we have **Team 1** working on a **Minimum Viable Product** (**MVP**) release at the end of Q4. Goals and milestones serve both as drivers and as revision points for our roadmap. Normally, we must revise the roadmap when we reach a milestone, regardless of whether it's been realized or not. Milestones need not only be internal to our product or organization. A milestone could be the release of a competitor's rival product or the introduction of some new market regulations. Any event that marks a clear achievement in our product's progress or affects our Product Goal is a milestone event.

> **Important Note**
>
> An MVP is a simplified version of our product that only contains those features considered sufficient for it to be of value to its users. For example, the popular website AirBnB's MVP was a simple website where users could rent one specific property in one specific location for a fixed term. This was subsequently expanded to include many properties all over the world and provided many rental options. MVPs are useful for gaining early adoption and validating a product idea early in the development cycle.

Above all, we should never forget the Agile and Scrum principles when creating product roadmaps: empiricism is the basis that we operate on. Everything changes and we must adjust to changes rather than stubbornly stick to plans that have been overwritten by reality. As Mike Tyson famously said:

Everyone has a plan until they get punched in the mouth.

During product development, it is likely that we will metaphorically get punched in the mouth more than once. Sticking to a plan that gets us punched is not a very good idea, which is why we should revise and adjust our roadmap often so that we can avoid any incoming mishaps. If we have a realistic and regularly revised roadmap and can give reliable estimates, we can start making forecasts about our work. We'll explore this next.

Forecasting with velocity and burn charts

We can't really create any kind of plan without forecasting the impact of our work. For instance, during Sprint planning, we are called to decide on how many Product Backlog items we can work on during the Sprint. This is impossible to do without having some prior knowledge of our team's capacity or ability to deliver work. We usually employ the metric of velocity to forecast the work we can deal with during the Sprint. In addition, many Agile teams use burnup and burndown charts to track progress at any point during the Sprint. In this section, we'll examine these three metric concepts. Let's begin by understanding what velocity is all about.

Calculating team velocity

Velocity is a metric that specifies the average amount of Product Backlog items we can turn into an Increment during a Sprint. Having a sold estimation process, as described in the previous sections of this chapter, is essential in producing reliable velocity values. To measure velocity, we need to keep track of how many story points we are completing in each Sprint. So, if we have four items in our Sprint Backlog, estimated at five points each, and we get three of these items *done*, then we have completed 15 story points worth of work. Velocity is what is known in statistics as the *simple moving average* of our Done story points. For instance, if, in the last three Sprints, we completed four, eight, and six story points, respectively, then our velocity would be (4+8+6) / 3 = 6.

Let's look at a more detailed example:

Sprint	Done Story Points	Velocity
1	14	14
2	18	16
3	12	14
4	18	16
5	20	18

Figure 6.3 – Calculating velocity

The preceding table represents the last five Sprints. For the first Sprint, we had Done items worth **14** story points in total, so our moving average (that is, our velocity) is 14 / 1 = 14. In the second Sprint, we completed **18** points worth of *Done* items, so our velocity is now (14 + 18) / 2. In the third Sprint, our velocity changes to (14 + 18 + 12) / 3 = 14.6. In short, we calculate velocity by summing up all the previously Done story points and dividing the total by the number of Sprints.

> **Tip**
> It takes at least five Sprints to establish a reliable team velocity.

Now that we know what velocity is, let's look at an alternative way of calculating it. Using a single value to represent velocity can be limiting and may lead to inaccurate forecasts. A more flexible approach is to represent velocity in terms of confidence intervals, instead of as a single value. A **confidence interval** is a range of values that we are confident our velocity lies in.

> **Tip**
> A confidence interval is a statistical method that uses the standard deviation of a dataset to calculate different probabilities that the desired value will lie within certain ranges. If the dataset is our previously done story points per Sprint, then we can calculate a range of values to denote our estimated velocity with a certain degree of confidence that our estimate is accurate.

There are many free online calculators (such as `https://www.calculator.net/ confidence-interval-calculator`) where we can feed in our previous Sprint data and get a confidence interval for our velocity. So, if we process our [12, 14, 18, 18, 20] historical Sprint data for a 95% confidence interval, we will find that the range for this confidence interval is 15.7 – 20.2. This means that we are 95% certain our team's velocity falls within this range. Knowing this, we can be much more flexible when selecting Product Backlog items for our Sprint, as it's much easier matching estimated items to a range of values rather than a specific value.

So, we can calculate our velocity as either a single value representing the simple moving average or a range of values representing a confidence interval. Whichever way we choose to do this, we get a velocity metric that helps us forecast the amount of work we can do in a Sprint. At this point, we may also be wondering how we can track our progress during the Sprint or even over many Sprints. For this, we need to understand burn charts.

Burndown charts

Burndown charts let us visualize how much work has been done and how much work remains to be done. A burndown chart is a simple linear chart with two axes:

- A vertical axis, denoting the work to be done, usually in the form of story points.
- A horizontal axis, representing the remaining time. In the case of a daily Sprint chart, that would be represented as days.

To create a Sprint daily burndown chart, we must do the following:

1. On the vertical (work) axis, mark the story points we estimated for the Sprint.
2. On the horizontal (time) axis, mark the days of the Sprint.
3. Draw a straight line between the two points we marked previously. This will be the ideal burndown slope.
4. Every day during the Sprint, mark the amount of work that was completed on that day.
5. Join the daily work marks to form a line on the chart. This is the *actual* burndown slope.

Let's see at what a burndown chart looks like so that we can appreciate the aforementioned steps:

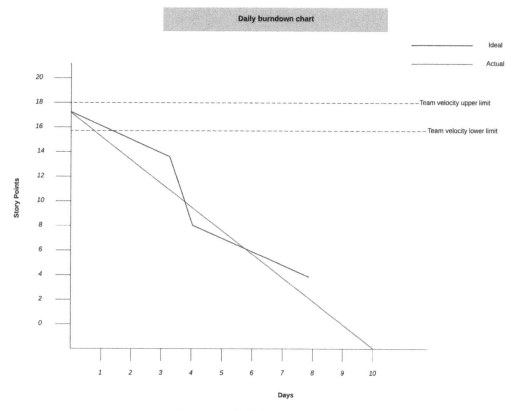

Figure 6.4 – Daily burndown chart

In the preceding chart, we can see that the team estimated 17 story points to be worked on during the Sprint. We can observe how, in the first 2 days of the Sprint, the team delivered about one story point per day; then, between days 3-4, the team delivered approximately sux story points worth of work. We can also see that we are currently on the eighth Sprint day (because that's the end of the *actual work* line) and that there are about four story points worth of work remaining.

> **Tip**
>
> We can use burndown charts for longer-term forecasting too. To do that, we must project the total story points estimated for a release (or some other goal, as defined on our product roadmap) on the vertical axis and the number of Sprints on the horizontal axis. Then, we must update the chart at the end of each Sprint with the story points that were completed for that Sprint.

Burndown charts are very useful for tracking remaining work, but they're not good at showing how much work has been completed and the total amount of work. For that, we need a burnup chart.

Burnup charts

Burnup charts are similar to burndown charts, in the sense that they are both linear charts. However, their usefulness and application are different. Burnup charts let us visualize progress over time. They are especially useful for tracking progress toward a longer-term goal, such as a release or another goal or milestone on our product roadmap. The vertical axis of the chart is for the total project work planned, while the horizontal axis is for tracking completed work.

To create a burnup chart for a goal, such as a Release, we must do the following:

1. On the vertical (work) axis, we mark the story points we estimated for the Release. This is our planned work line.

2. On the horizontal (time) axis, we mark the Sprints we have planned for the Release.

3. Draw a straight line from the point where our planned work line meets the final Sprint, all the way down to the start of the axis (point 0). This is the *ideal* line of completed work.

4. At the end of each Sprint, mark the amount of story points that were delivered during the Sprint.

5. Join the daily work marks to form a line on the chart. This is the *actual* line of completed work.

Let's look at a burnup chart:

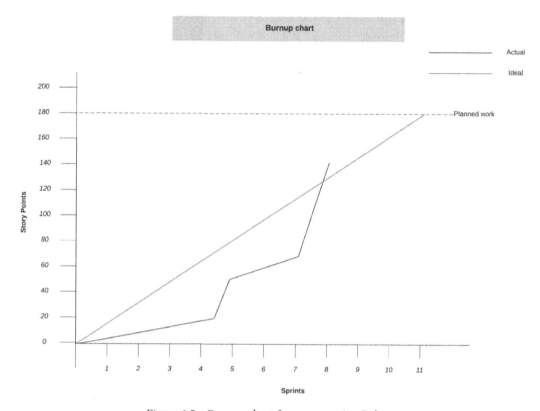

Figure 6.5 – Burnup chart for an upcoming Release

In this chart, we've estimated that the work items needed for our goal amount to 180 story points worth of work. We have 11 sprints planned to deliver this work, so we can calculate that we should be delivering, on average, 16.3 (180/11) story points per Sprint.

The blue line represents the actual number of story points that have been completed. We can see that for the first four Sprints, the team was making steady progress, then became very productive during the fifth Sprint, and then leveled off again. The blue line ends at the eighth Sprint, indicating we have three Sprints remaining to reach our goal. Roughly 37 story points are remaining to reach our planned work line. This burnup chart allows us to make some very useful inferences:

- If the planned work line has been raised halfway through the chart, this means that work has been added to our project. This is what is usually known as scope creep.

- If the ideal work line changes halfway through the chart, a change has been made to the original plan for how much work will be completed in each Sprint.

- If the actual work line is below the ideal work line, we are behind schedule.
- If the actual work line is above the ideal work line, we are ahead of schedule.

As we can see, burnup charts allow us to monitor team efficiency between Sprints. It helps us track how much work is left and whether we can expect to reach our goal on time, based on our progress. It also helps us see the impact any changes in scope have on our progress. We can use this to show our stakeholders how much longer the project should take if they want to add additional work.

Overall, both types of burn charts are useful in a complementary manner. Used together, they enable Scrum Teams to monitor and forecast progress, which is essential for managing product development.

Summary

In this chapter, we learned about estimation, planning, and forecasting. These skills are not part of the Scrum Guide and are not essential for passing the PSP I exam. However, they are skills that all Scrum Masters should possess to fully comprehend the product life cycle, and to best be able to provide leadership and counseling to the Scrum Team.

Due to this, we learned about how to estimate with story points by playing Planning Poker or using estimation buckets, as well as the different ways we can tweak these methods to our needs and circumstances. We also learned how to create a product roadmap and how this roadmap helps us formulate our Product Backlog and group our work into themes and capabilities (or epics).

Finally, we learned how to measure and monitor our progress and forecast our future work using velocity and burn charts. In the next chapter, we'll discuss how to manage the work that takes place within the Sprint. See you there!

Questions

1. Developers have estimated a Product Backlog item at 8 story points. Which of the following statements is true? (Choose one answer.)

   a) The item will require 8 working days to complete.

   b) The item is likely to take more effort or be more complex than an item estimated at 5 points.

   c) The item is too large or complex to be completed within a Sprint.

   d) The item will require 8 working hours to complete.

2. In what ways is the product roadmap useful? (Choose the three most appropriate answers.)

    a) It clearly identifies priorities and initiatives that should be pursued to realize the product goal.

    b) It sets specific dates for software releases in order to focus and motivate the Scrum team.

    c) It communicates the product strategy to external stakeholders.

    d) It demonstrates to stakeholders how we are going to realize the product goal as a series of activities leading to achievable milestones.

3. What do estimation techniques such as planning poker encourage exactly? (Choose one answer.)

    a) To follow the opinion of the lead developer.

    b) To satisfy the planning needs of the product owner.

    c) To reach a consensus by discussing the differences and reasons for individual estimates.

    d) To reach a consensus by developers voting on each other's estimates.

4. Which of the following statements about velocity is FALSE? (Choose one answer.)

    a) It indicates how much work developers can take on in a Sprint.

    b) It denotes the average number of story points that developers complete in a Sprint.

    c) It measures developers' productivity compared with another team of developers.

    d) It allows us to forecast our work into the future.

5. I want to visualize how much work has been done and how much work remains to be done in the Sprint. Which tool do I use? (Choose one answer.)

    a) A burn-up chart

    b) A burn-down chart

    c) The product roadmap

    d) The team's velocity

Further reading

- *Succeeding with Agile software development using Scrum, Mike Cohn, Addison-Wesley, 2009*

- *Introduction to the New Statistics: Estimation, Open Science, and Beyond, Geoff Cumming and Robert Calin-Jageman, 21 Oct. 2016*

7
The Sprint Journey

So far in this book, we have learned about the Scrum Team, events, and artifacts, things that form the basis of the Scrum framework. We also explored some standard practices used by Scrum Teams for planning and forecasting. What all of the aforementioned have in common is that they take place or interact with each other during the main Scrum Event, that is, the **Sprint**. The Sprint is a container event, within which the Scrum Team selects, plans, and delivers value in the form of one (or more) increments.

In this chapter, we'll discuss the activities that take place inside a Sprint, beyond and in addition to the previously examined Scrum Events. Specifically, we will learn how to deal with all the things that take place within the Sprint, such as the following:

- Refining the Product Backlog
- Preparing for the first Sprint
- Monitoring progress with a Scrum Board
- What to do when the Sprint Goal is not achieved
- Managing defects
- Canceling the Sprint

By the end of the chapter, you should know how to start your first Sprint, what to do when common eventualities occur within the Sprint, and your role and responsibilities as a Scrum Master. Let's start by learning how to refine the Product Backlog.

Refining the Product Backlog

Before we can start a Sprint, we must have a refined Product Backlog. Product Backlog refinement is the activity of breaking down backlog items into more concise and manageable items and providing more details. During refining, the Scrum Team analyzes, discusses, estimates, and orders backlog items. The purpose of the activity is to enable Developers to start working on items with the least amount of disruption or ambiguity.

So, a refined backlog is one in which items are detailed, estimated, and ordered. We have already learned how to create detailed and descriptive backlog items as user stories or features in *Chapter 5, Scrum Artifacts*. We have also examined how to estimate items in *Chapter 6, Planning and Estimating with Scrum*. In this section, we'll delve more into the one remaining aspect of backlog refinement we haven't covered yet: **ordering**.

> Tip
>
> Some Scrum Teams hold weekly **refinement meetings**, usually led by the **Product Owner (PO)**. This is not a bad practice in itself; however, it may lead to the false impression that the PO is solely responsible for the backlog refinement. This is not true. Although the PO has the final say on Product Backlog items, the whole team is responsible for refining those items. If, for instance, a Developer acquires some new information about an item, they should share that information with the team as soon as practically possible. Refinement is a continuous process, shared by the whole team, and should not be limited just to regular meetings.

Ordering a backlog may seem a simple matter of prioritizing the most urgent items, but it's actually much subtler than that. Let's take a closer look.

Learning how to apply order to the Product Backlog

When ordering a backlog, we usually place the higher-order items at the top of the backlog. The ordering of the items may be done in different ways. There are four main criteria to consider when ordering the backlog:

- **Value**: This is about the benefits an item provides to the stakeholders, the organization, or the Team. These could be of business or economic value. It is common to order higher-value requirements first. For example, if we're working in the financial domain, we would expect items that describe how to move money around to be at the top of our backlog. If we're building a shopping product, our stakeholders would want to see items pertaining to shopping list, basket, and payment functionalities at the top of the backlog. Such items are essential to converting and retaining customers, that is, they are high-value items.

- **Cost**: Cost ordering is about implementing items that can be delivered with the least time, effort, or money (the *low-hanging fruit* approach). It can also be about delivering items with the greatest **return on investment** (**ROI**). ROI is usually calculated by dividing the estimated value of an item by its estimated cost. For instance, a backlog item that would take most of the Sprint to implement but would make our product more accessible to new customers would be said to have a high ROI rating.

- **Risk**: Ordering based on risk is most used on products leveraging new, controversial, or disruptive ideas or technologies. The idea is that, if the high-risk items fail to be delivered, then the product can be scaled down or re-scoped.

- **Urgency**: Some items may be more time-sensitive than others. For instance, an item might be defining some functionality that is scheduled for demonstration at an upcoming trade show or conference. Such an item would find its way to the top of the product backlog, to be implemented at the next Sprint.

The way to determine which of these criteria is the most appropriate when ordering an item is to view our backlog in the context of the Product Roadmap, as discussed in *Chapter 6*, *Planning and Estimation with Scrum*. The state of our product development is in relation to the roadmap allows us to establish whether risk, urgency, cost, or value will be driving the order of the Product Backlog, at that point in time. The Scrum Master plays an important role in helping the team with backlog refinement.

Scrum Master duties for Product Backlog refinement

The Scrum Master plays a vital role in Product Backlog refinement. They must create transparency on all levels and educate and inform the team, as needed. The Scrum Master should do the following:

- Facilitate Product Backlog refinement workshops.

- Ensure the three aspects of Product Backlog refinement (detail, estimates, and order) are fully understood by the team.

- Communicate the importance of shared responsibility when refining the backlog.

- Teach Developers best practices for estimating items.

- Help the team in scoping or breaking up backlog items in such a way that an item can be delivered (**Done**) within a Sprint.

Another important part of the Scrum Master's duties is to ensure the team gives Product Backlog refinement the attention it deserves. It's a common occurrence for some teams not to devote enough time or energy to refinement, as their attention is on the Sprint.

But making time for regular and collaborative Product Backlog refinement can make the difference between a successful and a mediocre product.

Knowing how to detail, estimate, and order the Product Backlog items will ensure that the most fitting items get added to the Sprint Backlog. This is essential for the Scrum team to keep delivering the right value at the right time. So, now that we know how to refine our Product Backlog, let's look at another way to ensure our Sprint is successful.

Preparing for the first Sprint

In Scrum, every Sprint is treated exactly the same as any other Sprint. It is a time-boxed event in which the Scrum Team delivers value by creating an increment of potentially releasable software. No Sprint is *special* in that respect. Some teams, however, especially teams inexperienced in Scrum, tend to treat the first Sprint a bit differently than the others.

> **Tip**
> Avoid the *Scrum 0* anti-pattern. A **Scrum 0** is a Scrum dedicated to setting up infrastructure, creating a design or architecture, initial backlog refinements, and other preparatory work. Scrum 0 is just a set of preliminary activities and does not produce an increment of potentially releasable software. Sprints designed not to produce a Done increment undermine the Scrum principles and should not be pursued.

A common misconception about the first Sprint is that because it's not expected to produce user-side functionality, then it's a *special* Sprint and can be used as a repository for all other activities, as described earlier. This is not true. The key here is understanding what *potentially releasable software* means. It doesn't necessarily mean fully functional or even user-facing software, though some people perceive it that way. It just means *Done* software that can be released to the stakeholders if the Product Owner decides it adds value to do so. A skeleton web application (commonly known as **scaffolding**) that simply prints **hello world** on screen, is *potentially releasable software* if it meets the definition of Done. Whether it will be worth releasing to the stakeholders is a different matter. The point is, to put it in simple terms, that the Sprint produces software that works and helps accomplish the Sprint Goal. If the Sprint Goal is to create a basic website that we can enhance later, then our *hello world* site is a perfectly good increment.

Before embarking on product development and starting the Sprint cycle, the Scrum Team must do some preparation. This includes the following:

- Discussing and understanding the product to be developed. This is better done with the aid of the Product Roadmap, as described in *Chapter 6, Planning and Estimating with Scrum*. This discussion may also lead to some initial decisions about the product's architecture and design.

- Agreeing on the Sprint length. This will obviously be an educated guess because, prior to starting development, it is impossible to know the optimal Sprint length for the specific product and team. A 2-week Sprint length is usually a safe bet to start with. The Sprint length can always be adjusted at a later Sprint Retrospective event (see *Chapter 4, Scrum Events*).

- Initial Product Backlog refinement, as discussed in the previous section of this chapter. This will provide the team with some detailed and ordered backlog items that can be included in the first Sprint Backlog.

- Creating the infrastructure needed for product development. This will mean different things, dependent on the team, product, and organization. It may include a range of different actions, from purchasing new laptops and setting up AWS/Azure accounts, to acquiring software licenses and many more things.

- A definition of Done, as discussed in *Chapter 5, Scrum Artifacts*.

A very important thing to remember during this preparatory phase is that *in Scrum, empiricism rules*. No decision taken during these initial stages is set in stone. Infrastructure, architecture, tools, and design are all subject to change if it is later found that they do not help the team's productivity. All these things should be inspected during Sprint Retrospectives and changed if necessary.

So, now that we know how to begin our first Sprint, let's take a look at the things we need to do within the Sprint.

Tracking progress with a Scrum Board

A **Scrum Board** is a tool that helps Scrum Teams visualize Sprint Backlog items and track their progress. The board can have different styles and content, depending on the team and organization where it's being used, but its purpose remains the same. The board is updated by the team and shows all items that need to be completed for the current Sprint. Items on a Scrum Board are usually represented as cards. Each card has a title, description, and other metadata, and can be colored and labeled in different ways.

Scrum Boards are not strictly defined. Some have fewer columns than others. Some have differently named columns. What they all have in common, however, is that they allow us to visualize our workflow, to know how our team is doing, and to get a feel for the direction our development is heading. A minimalist Scrum Board is depicted in the following diagram:

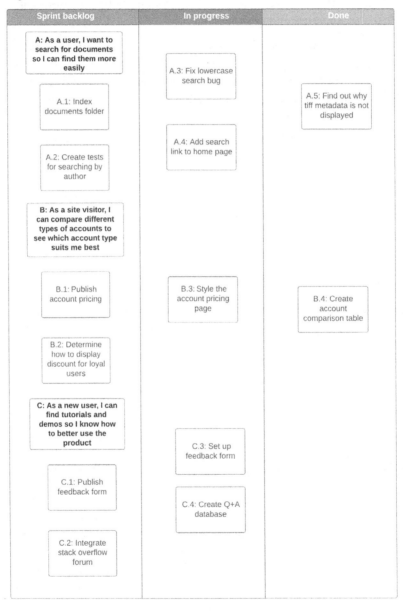

Figure 7.1 – A Scrum Board

Let's examine the board's columns more closely:

- **Sprint backlog**: This is where we place the Product Backlog items that we have committed to deliver in the Sprint, during the Sprint Planning event. All the items placed in the Sprint Backlog will have been described in detail, estimated, and have clear acceptance criteria. This is where we also place the tasks required to implement and deliver the Product Backlog items. These tasks are not restricted to programming but may represent anything necessary to deliver the item. For example, a task may involve retrieving some information from a stakeholder or writing some documentation. We place all these tasks in the **Sprint Backlog** column.

- **In progress**: Tasks that we've started working on are moved into this column. They stay here until they are **Done**.

- **Done**: When a task has been completed and meets our definition of **Done**, it is moved to the **Done** column. For coding tasks, this would usually mean that the code passes all tests and has been code-reviewed.

As we can see in the diagram, we have selected a number of Product Backlog items (A, B, and C) for our Sprint Backlog. We have also created a number of tasks needed to deliver each item. So in the case of item A, we have created tasks A.1, A.2, A.3, and so on. When we start working on a task, for instance, A.3, we move it to the **In progress** column. We may also move the relevant item, A, to the **In progress** column too. Alternatively, we may wait until all A-related tasks have been moved off the **Sprint backlog** column before we move item A too. Choose whichever approach works best for your team.

As already mentioned, this is a simplified Scrum Board. Real-life Scrum Boards contain more columns than this. For instance, some teams like to indicate tasks that are code-complete but not code-reviewed in a separate column, before moving them to **Done**. Others prefer to have a **Staged** or **Deployed** column, where they place items deployed to the staging environment. There is no right or wrong way to structure a Scrum Board. Scrum Teams should adapt their board in a way that helps and reflects their own workflow.

> **Tip**
> The Scrum Master should help the team choose the best Scrum Board layout that reflects the team's cadence and needs.

Items on the Scrum Board are moved between columns by the Developers during the Sprint. It's the responsibility of the Developer working on the item to move it to the next column, when required.

Ultimately, a Scrum Board will be used in the same manner: to ensure board items are moved from left to right. At the start of the Sprint, the leftmost column (**Sprint backlog**) will be the only populated one, while the others are empty. At the end of a completed Sprint, the rightmost (**Done**) column should be full while the rest are empty. This raises the question, *What happens when at the end of the Sprint we haven't managed to deliver all the Sprint Backlog items?* Let's examine this scenario next.

What to do when the Sprint Goal is not achieved

Occasionally, the team will realize they are not able to reach the Sprint Goal by the end of the Sprint or that the Goal hasn't been achieved at the end of Sprint. This usually happens because of two reasons:

- The Developers haven't been able to deliver all the Sprint Backlog items.

- The increment is not in a usable state.

Let's examine both causes, starting with the first one. When one or more Sprint Backlog items have not been finished by the end of the Sprint, this is sometimes due to extraneous circumstances (for example, a Developer has fallen ill). Most often, however, it happens because the Developers did not estimate the items correctly. Unfinished items by the Sprint's end are not uncommon, although this tends to happen more often during the early Sprints, when the team hasn't yet established its internal rhythm and delivery cadence.

> **Important note**
>
> Some teams and organizations refer to Sprints that didn't achieve the Sprint Goal as **failed** Sprints. This is a counterproductive characterization that goes against the spirit and values of Scrum. The purpose of a Sprint is to provide a time-box within which the team can deliver value, as described by an overarching Sprint Goal. It's not to be used as a checkbox for a manager to mark as failure or success.

The second cause is when the delivered increment is not in good working order. This could mean that the code we delivered does not behave as intended, due to code bugs, design flaws, or even misunderstood requirements. Whatever the cause is, we must understand exactly why the increment is not acceptable to the stakeholders. Most of the time, this occurs because of subtle coding defects that weren't detected during standard testing. In such cases, a simple solution might be to extend our definition of *Done* with a step for having all code run through a static analyzer, linter, or other QA tool.

The Scrum framework provides opportunities to detect when our Sprint starts veering off-goal. The Daily Scrum (see *Chapter 4, Scrum Events*) and the burn-down chart (see *Chapter 6, Planning and Estimating with Scrum*) allow us to determine whether and when we'll be able to complete the Sprint. So, what do we do when we are in the last few days of the Sprint and it has become obvious that we won't be able to deliver all Sprint Backlog items or that the increment we have delivered is not good enough? The truth is that there is no prescribed way of managing such occurrences; different Scrum teams deal with this in different ways. Having said that, in such a case, the following steps should serve you well:

1. **Root cause analysis**: The Developers need to find out why they weren't able to complete the Sprint. Was it a case of underestimating, changed circumstances, or unmitigated risks? Whatever the root cause was, it must be discovered and documented, for future reference and avoidance.

2. **Re-estimation**: The Developers must document the remaining work for any incomplete item and re-estimate accordingly.

3. **Moving incomplete items back to the Product Backlog**: Some Developers may be tempted to just leave any affected items in the Sprint Backlog, ready for the next Sprint, but that's not an appropriate response. Items should only be placed in the Sprint Backlog with the consensus of the whole Scrum Team, and that includes the Product Owner. For that reason, incomplete items must be moved back to the Product Backlog. In the Sprint Planning event for the next Sprint, the Product Owner will prioritize the item and the whole team will decide whether to put in in the upcoming Sprint's backlog.

4. **Discussing the item at the Sprint Retrospective**: This is what Sprint Retrospectives are for. This is where the root cause analysis we initially performed comes into play. We discuss what went wrong and how we can avoid it happening in the future. If the delivered increment was not in working condition, this is where we try to understand why and re-evaluate our definition of *Done*. The Sprint Retrospective is an opportunity for learning and improving as a team.

Let's look at an example of a Sprint where the Sprint Goal has not been achieved, as depicted in the following Scrum Board:

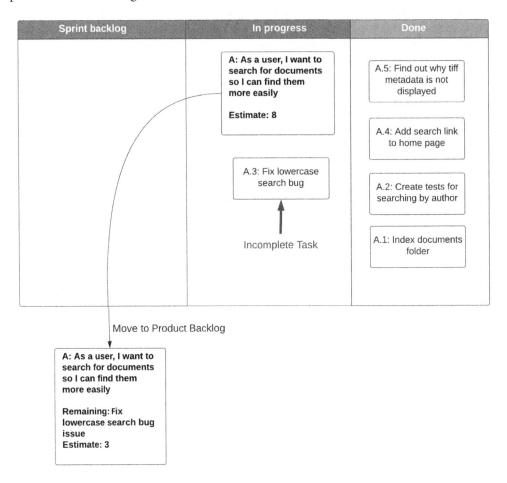

Figure 7.2 – Scrum Board for an incomplete Sprint

The preceding Scrum Board depicts our work progress at the end of the Sprint. The Developers were working on one item (**Search for documents**), which they broke down as five separate tasks. One of these tasks (**Fix lowercase search bug**) was not done by the end of the Sprint. The Developers know what needs to be done for this task, but they didn't have the time to do it during the Sprint. So, they document the remaining work for that item and set a new estimate for it. The item was initially estimated as an **8**, but with most of the work done, it is now estimated as a **3**. The item is now moved back to the Product Backlog, where the Product Owner will order the item and the whole Scrum Team will decide whether to include it in the next Sprint. They also add the item to the agenda for discussion at the Sprint Retrospective.

So, what happens to our team velocity in the scenario we just discussed? Do we add the 8 story-points we originally estimated for the incomplete item to our Sprint's total of story-points? There are differing opinions on the matter. Some Scrum Teams take the strict approach: if an item is not completed (or is causing an increment to be rejected), the Developers should not be credited with the story-points for that item. I find this a bit harsh and unrepresentative of the actual work performed and value delivered. I tend to prefer a different allocation of story-points: after the item has been re-estimated, the Developers are credited with the *median* points between the original and re-estimated value. Consider our previous example. The incomplete item was originally estimated to represent 8 story-points (on a Fibonacci scale). It was placed back on the Product Backlog and re-estimated to be 3 story-points, since much of the work for it has already been done. The Developers will be credited with 5 story-points (1, 3, 5, 8) worth of work. This is a fairer reflection of the work the Developers already performed for that item and helps establish a more accurate velocity reading in the long term.

Managing defects

Defects are an unavoidable part of software development. No one is perfect and no methodology is foolproof; as a result, every Scrum Team will deal with defects at some time during product development. Scrum provides plenty of opportunities for inspection and adaptation, thereby helping to take steps to minimize the occurrence and impact of defects. The way we deal with defects in Scrum depends largely on when the defects are discovered:

- *In-Sprint* defects are defects discovered within the current Sprint.
- *Out-of-Sprint* defects are discovered in previously released increments.

Before delving into these two scenarios, let's talk a bit more about defects.

Knowing how to triage defects

A defect is a discrepancy between the software's actual and expected behavior. A defect is usually caused by a coding or design error (a bug) or by a misunderstanding of the user requirements. When the Scrum Team becomes aware of a defect, they should ensure that the defect is appropriately triaged. This involves determining two basic attributes of the defect:

- **Priority** is about the timeframe by which the defect must be fixed. This usually determined by business or client needs, such as release dates, **service level agreements** (**SLAs**), planned presentations, and others. A defect's priority is usually rated as *low, medium*, or *high*.

- **Severity** is about quantifying the impact of the defect on the product's users. This is normally determined by the functionality area and the number of users affected. For example, a defect with a shopping application's basket checkout functionality would be classed as critically severe as it affects a core system area and most of the application's users. A defect's severity is usually rated as *critical, major, moderate, minor,* and *cosmetic.*

A defect's priority and severity are not always correlated. A defect may have a high severity but low priority, or a low severity and high priority. Consider an example where a defect affecting some functionality is rated as moderate as it only affects very specific usage scenarios. However, our organization has committed to presenting this functionality to a trade conference next week. The defect then would be given the highest priority, meaning it has to be fixed as soon as possible.

When a defect is detected, the Scrum Team should create a backlog item to represent it. If the team employs user stories to define the backlog items, then they should create a story to describe the defect, together with acceptance criteria for fixing it. Let's start by looking at how to manage defects that occur within the Sprint.

Dealing with defects in the current Sprint

This is the easiest defect-related situation to deal with, as the defect can be managed within the Sprint and without affecting the Sprint Goal or greatly disrupting current work. Usually, we find defects in our code when we test it, or when the code gets *code-reviewed*. With these, we simply create a task to fix the defect and move on. The defect is dealt with during our normal work cadence, that is, the defective item is already in the **In progress** column and stays there until the defect is fixed. Sometimes, though, we find defects in code that has been **Finished** or **Done**.

Here's a not-uncommon scenario: midway through the Sprint, the Developers deliver a Sprint Backlog item, which meets the definition of Done. The item is moved onto the **Done** column of the Scrum Board. The code is automatically deployed to a staging server, where other Developers or the Product Owner can use it. But when they do so, they discover that the code doesn't work the way it should. In this case, the Developers should follow these steps:

1. Move the defective item back to the **In progress** column.

2. Create a new task to fix the defect.

3. Embellish the item's description and acceptance criteria, if necessary.

4. Change the definition of **Done** at the Sprint Retrospective.

The following diagram illustrates this scenario:

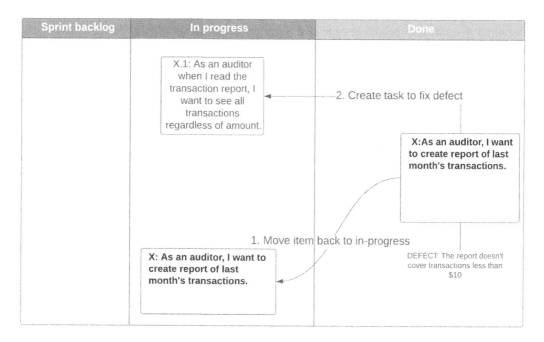

Figure 7.3 – Managing in-Sprint defects with Done items

Here, developer Alice finishes the transaction report item and moves it to the **Done** column. Bob, another Developer, runs the code as part of testing a related item he is working on. He observes that the report is missing transactions below a certain amount. He notifies Alice of the problem, who then proceeds to move the item back to the **In progress** column and creates a task to address the defect. Alice may also consider adding some more acceptance criteria to the item or some extra tests in the code, so as to ensure similar defects are avoided in the future. When the defect is fixed and verified, then Alice can move the transactions report item (X) and the defect item (X.1) back to the **Done** column. The Developers must make a note to review the definition of **Done** at the Sprint Retrospective as to avoid similar problems re-occurring.

Dealing with in-Sprint defects is usually a straightforward situation. Things get a bit more complex when we must deal with out-of-Sprint defects. Let's examine this scenario.

Dealing with defects from previous Sprints

Here is another common scenario: in the last Sprint, we successfully delivered an increment that was subsequently released to our external stakeholders. We have now started working on a new Sprint. However, the stakeholders complain of a defect in our released increment. In this case, we manage the defect thus:

1. The Scrum Team creates a new Product Backlog item to describe the defect.

2. The Product Owner, in consultation with the stakeholders, triages the defect as described in the *Knowing how to triage defects* section.

3. The Product Owner orders the item in the Product Backlog according to its triaged priority and severity. The Scrum Team can then decide whether to include the item in the next Sprint's backlog during the next Sprint Planning event.

There is an extreme case of this scenario, where the defect is so severe and time-critical that it must be fixed right now, in the current Sprint. There is often great pressure from the organization and senior managers to do so. This goes against the Scrum principles, as discussed in *Chapter 2, Scrum Theory and Principles*. It can, however, be done, with certain conditions:

- The Scrum Master must emphasize to the organization that this practice affects the team's productivity, the product development, and the team's predictive and forecasting ability. It is therefore something that should not be occurring often.

- The Sprint Backlog must be re-balanced. That means that the defect's size and complexity must be estimated, and an equivalent number of items must be removed from the Sprint Backlog. This may cause the Sprint Goal to be re-scoped or, in the worst case, be made redundant (we'll discuss this further in the following section, *Canceling the Sprint*).

Overall, dealing with previous defects in the current Sprint is a risky and disruptive practice that should be avoided wherever possible. The safest approach is to add the defect to the Product Backlog, where it can be analyzed, discussed, estimated, and added to the next Sprint Backlog. Now, since we're talking about risky and disruptive practices, it would be a good time to examine another scenario that will cause great disruption: canceling the Sprint.

Canceling the Sprint

A Sprint may end in one of two ways. The vast majority of times, the Team will have worked throughout the Sprint's duration and will have ended up achieving, not achieving, or partly achieving the Sprint Goal. We have already discussed how to deal with these eventualities in the previous sections of this chapter. However, there are some very rare occasions where the team won't get to the end of the Sprint, as the Sprint gets canceled. Let's examine this more closely.

Canceling a Sprint is a very rare phenomenon. It generally happens when a new situation or extraordinary circumstances shift the team's commitment and focus. A Sprint must not get canceled if the Scrum Team simply decides that it cannot complete the work, or that it cannot reach the Sprint Goal. Frequently canceled Sprints should ring alarm bells. They may be a sign that the Scrum Team is lacking focus and commitment, the product is lacking a vision, or the organization does not appreciate the Scrum values and principles.

> **Important note**
> A Sprint should be canceled only if the Sprint Goal becomes obsolete. The only person who can decide to cancel the Sprint is the Product Owner.

A cancellation could occur when, for example, the team is working on a Sprint with a Goal to deliver a new, unique product feature when a competitor company releases the same feature on their product. The Product Owner, in conjunction with the stakeholders, may then decide that there is no longer any point in trying to reach that Sprint Goal and cancel the Sprint.

What to do with the Sprint Backlog items

If there are **Done** items when the Sprint is canceled, then the Product Owner may decide to do either of the following:

- Throw them away, if the items offer no business value, under the new circumstances.
- If the items still represent valuable work, then keep the work to produce an increment that can be released at a later date.

Any items that haven't been **Done** when the Sprint is canceled should be re-estimated and put back in the Product Backlog.

How to wrap up a canceled Sprint

Some Scrum Teams prefer to have a Sprint Retrospective after a canceled Sprint, regardless. Others prefer to carry it to the next Sprint's Retrospective. It doesn't really matter, as long as the team has a chance to inspect and adapt according to what happened in the Sprint.

If the team has some free time because of the cancellation, for instance if the Sprint was canceled on a Wednesday and the next Sprint isn't due to start until Monday, then the team should decide how to best spend the remaining time. A good use of that time might be to do some Product Backlog refinement, as per the first section of this chapter, but it's up to a self-managing team to manage its own time.

We'll finish this section by restating that Sprint cancellations carry a heavy price on team productivity and morale, create waste, and are often more trouble than they're worth, so do your best to avoid canceling a Sprint, if possible.

Summary

In this chapter, we learned about managing the Sprint itself. Practices for refining the backlog, using a Scrum Board, or managing defects are not part of the Scrum framework and aren't explained in the Scrum Guide. However, they are vital parts of a Sprint and essential knowledge for a skilled Scrum Master.

The first thing we learned is how to order the Product Backlog. A properly ordered backlog makes adding items to the Sprint Backlog so much easier and optimizes the value delivered in the Sprint. We then examined how to prepare the team for the beginning of product development and the first Sprint. Getting prepared before the Sprint development cycle begins ensures that the first Sprint will go smoothly and that the Scrum values and principles are not compromised.

Next, we discussed how to use a Scrum Board to track our progress through the Sprint and how to cope with different scenarios, such as when defects are found or when the Sprint Goal cannot be achieved. We also covered the unlikely scenario of having to cancel the Sprint. Knowing how to respond to such eventualities in an organized and adaptive manner ensures high team productivity and reduces the risk of derailing the development cycle.

In the next chapter, we'll continue examining some more practical aspects of being a Scrum Master, such as getting familiar with release pipelines, scaling Scrum, and applying Scrum in remote teams. Keep reading!

Questions

1. Which activities are performed during Product Backlog refinement? (Choose all that apply.)

    a) Estimating backlog items

    b) Ordering backlog items

    c) Analyzing, discussing, and explaining backlog items

    d) Creating tasks required to complete backlog items

2. In which ways is the Product Backlog ordered? (Choose one answer.)

    a) Items with the highest value go to the top.

    b) Items with the lowest cost go to the top.

    c) Items with the lowest risk go to the top.

    d) Whichever way the product owner decides.

3. Certain Sprints, such as the first Sprint, are treated differently as they do not produce a Product Increment (TRUE or FALSE)

    a) True

    b) False

4. When should a Sprint be canceled? (Choose one answer.)

    a) Never. A Sprint should always be completed.

    b) When two or more developers are ill or otherwise absent.

    c) When the Sprint goal becomes redundant.

    d) When developers cannot complete the items in the Sprint Backlog.

5. During the Sprint, a defect is discovered related to an item currently in the 'in-progress' column of the Scrum board. What do you do? (Choose one answer.)

    a) Create a new card to capture the defect and add it to the Sprint Backlog column.

    b) Create a new card to capture the defect and add it to the Product Backlog.

    c) Don't create any new cards; just fix the defect quietly and move on.

    d) Call a team meeting to discuss the situation.

Further reading

- *Zombie Scrum Survival Guide (The Professional Scrum Series), Christiaan Verwijs, Johannes Schartau, Barry Overeem, Aug 2020*

- *Essential Scrum: A Practical Guide to the Most Popular Agile Process, Kenneth S. Rubin, Addison-Wesley, Jul 2012*

8
Facets of Scrum

In the previous chapter, we learned about practices and processes that we can apply within the **Sprint**. In this chapter, we'll apply the same principle at a higher, more generic level. We will learn practices and techniques that improve the development lifecycle, and also the quality of the product and the Scrum applications as a whole.

The following topics will be covered in this chapter:

- Learning software development practices for Scrum
- Leveraging testing methods for Scrum
- Applying Scrum to remote teams
- Managing technical debt
- Scaling Scrum

By the end of the chapter, you will know what a CI/CD pipeline is and how it helps the Scrum Team. You will also know what types of testing need to be applied at different levels of the CI/CD pipeline and how this affects the **Sprint planning**. You will also learn how to manage technical debt, apply Scrum in remote teams, and what to do when needing to use Scrum on large and complex products. Let's begin by looking at some software development practices suited for Scrum.

Learning software development practices for Scrum

Scrum inherently supports an iterative and incremental development cycle. A Sprint is an iteration during which the Scrum Team produces a potentially shippable increment. A Product Increment is working and usable software that is built on top of other increments. This is a powerful approach that enables constant and focused releases while allowing for constant inspection, adaptation, and transparency (see *Chapter 2, Scrum Theory and Principles*).

To make the most out of this cycle of short and focused *develop-build-release* cycles, which is the Sprint, we need to adopt software development practices that are best suited to it. In this section, we'll learn about source control models and the importance of continuous integration, deployment, and delivery.

Source control model for continuous integration

The issue of how to control and manage different versions of the same source code has existed since software developers started working together to create software applications. The current de facto standard for source and version control management in the software industry is **Git** (`https://git-scm.com`). Git is a distributed version control system, meaning that it allows concurrent development without relying on a central node or person for access and permissions. Git is an open source software tool that can be used to implement different build and control models.

These are called the **branching models**, as Git leverages a tree metaphor, where separate code versions are in fact branches sprouting off the main product code (the tree). Developers avoid overriding each other's changes by creating their own copy of the code base (a **branch**), while the main copy is called the **trunk** (also known as the master branch or mainline). When a developer wants to incorporate their branch back into the trunk, they use a process called **merging**. Each merge is based on specific points or snapshots of the trunk, called **code commits**.

There are many branching models that can be applied when using Git, such as **GitFlow**, feature branching, and others, but one of the simplest models and also most suitable to Scrum is **trunk-based development**. This works as depicted in the following diagram:

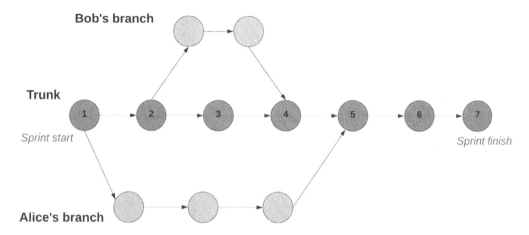

Figure 8.1 – Git trunk-based development

Let's suppose we are beginning a Sprint. Alice and Bob are both developers working on different coding tasks. Alice will create a branch off the trunk code base and work on it until her task is done, which involves three code commits (the circles on the diagram).

By the time she finishes, other developers, such as Bob, have already merged their own branches to the trunk, which now consists of four commits. Alice merges her branch back into the trunk as the fifth commit. By the end of the Sprint, all the branches have been merged into the trunk and the trunk has advanced by six commits. These six commits are the increment that we are delivering for that Sprint.

This practice of merging code changes back to the main branch as often as possible is called **continuous integration** (**CI**). It helps to avoid integration issues that often arise when infrequently merging code changes into the trunk. CI is the first step in a trio of software practices that are frequently used by Scrum Teams. The other two are **continuous delivery** and **continuous deployment**. Let's examine these next.

Continuous delivery and continuous deployment

Continuous delivery (**CD**) is an extension of CI. It involves automatically deploying all code changes to a staging or pre-production environment after the build stage. This is achieved by implementing an automated release process that can deploy our increment any time on the click of a button.

With CD, we get the benefit of having our increment automatically built and running on an environment closely emulating the production environment. This gives us great confidence in our development cadence and allows us to spot defects early. It also makes it easier to release increments to our stakeholders and customers. Since we have constant automated deployment to a staging environment, we are only one small step away from releasing our software to the production environment. Actually, this is where continuous deployment comes into play.

Continuous deployment goes one step further than CD. With this practice, every change that's successfully deployed to staging is automatically released to the stakeholders and customers. Continuous deployment removes the effort and stress of releasing increments at predetermined milestones or dates. The developers can focus on building software, while their work is constantly released to customers for review and feedback. The following diagram illustrates the differences between continuous integration, delivery, and deployment:

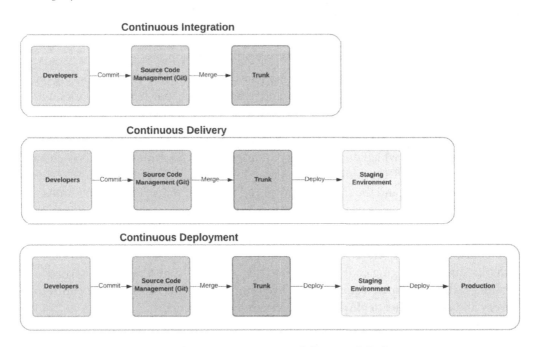

Figure 8.2 – Continuous integration, delivery, and deployment

The preceding diagram depicts the chain of activities that take the code from a development to a production environment. We call this chain a **build & release pipeline**, or a **CI/CD pipeline**. As you can see, the main differences between CI and CD are the addition of the deploying activities to staging and production environments, which are automatic. These are triggered when some quality assurance criterion, such as successful testing, is met. Testing actually plays a crucial part in establishing a CI/CD pipeline, such as the one depicted in the preceding diagram.

So now that we have learned about the CI source control model, CD, and continuous deployment, let's take a closer look at some useful testing practices in the next section.

Leveraging testing methods for Scrum

Testing is a very important part of the development process. In the old waterfall days, testing was something that was done usually just once, just before the code was to be released to the customers. It was performed by a dedicated testing team, which would test the code produced by the developers.

With Scrum, all this has changed. Now, testing is at the forefront of development and there is no distinction between software developers and testers. Scrum Developers are responsible for the full development cycle and this includes testing. Most Scrum Developers employ the **test-driven development** (**TDD**) paradigm (`https://developer.ibm.com/devpractices/software-development/articles/5-steps-of-test-driven-development/`).

In a nutshell, this means that developers write tests before they start writing code. The tests are created to specify and validate what the code does. Test cases for each functionality are developed and applied often to the working code. If the test fails, then the code is adjusted or rewritten in order to pass the test. There are different types of testing, each with a specific approach and goals. Let's examine some of them:

- **Unit testing**: This is the simplest and most regularly used form of testing. This is used to test a single unit of code, such as a class or function.

- **API/service testing**: This is about testing the interface between different code components or services.

- **Acceptance testing**: Used to verify acceptance criteria of user stories or executable specifications in the **Gherkin** (`https://cucumber.io/docs/guides/overview/`) specification language.

- **System testing**: This consists of end-to-end testing of the system to ensure it meets the requirements and functions according to specifications. System testing is applied to validate both functional and non-functional requirements, such as performance or accessibility.

- **Regression testing**: This is a combination of system and unit testing. It is applied to ensure that the added product functionality has not affected previous or existing functionality.

- **User acceptance testing**: This is a more informal testing method, where customers or users of the application try to perform their usual workflows or go through a user journey on the released application.

- **Smoke testing**: This is a short and quick testing method that checks the basic functionality of the application. This is usually applied after a release, to ensure that the major features of the application are working as expected.

Now that we understand the different levels of testing, let's see how this relates to the automated CI/CD pipeline we discussed in the previous section. The following diagram illustrates the types of testing needed at the CI and CD levels:

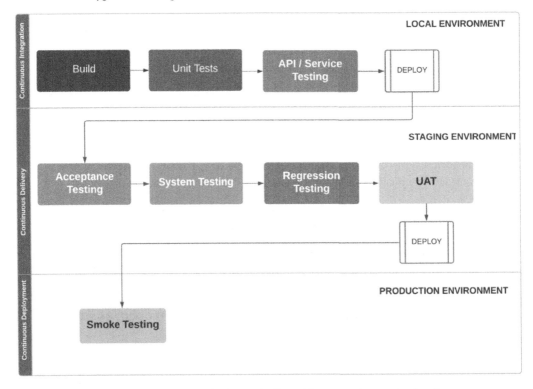

Figure 8.3 – Automated release pipeline with appropriate testing levels

To optimize the value delivered during a Sprint, all the activities in the preceding diagram should be automated. Software should be built at the click of a button and then fed through the testing and deployment steps of the pipeline until it is released to the end users (pending the Product Owner's consent or approval). This leaves the developers free and focused on working on Sprint Backlog items, while ensuring a constant feedback loop and minimizing defects.

As well as being important for the implementation of an automated release pipeline, testing levels knowledge also helps with the Sprint Planning event and the definition of Done. Let's assume that the definition of Done states, for instance, that software is only done once it is deployed on the staging environment and passes acceptance testing. The developers then will have to take into account the effort to implement the appropriate types of testing when estimating the backlog items, during Sprint Planning or Product Backlog refining.

In this section, we discussed the value of implementing a CI/CD pipeline when working with Scrum. We learned how a simple source version control model and appropriate types of testing help us continuously build, integrate, and deliver software within a Sprint.

In addition, the automated process of continuously building and delivering software becomes increasingly valuable when the Scrum Team is not physically co-located. Let's discuss what that involves in the next section.

Applying Scrum to remote teams

When Scrum was first conceptualized, software teams were co-located. Most of the Scrum Events were predicated on the team coming together in a room and using shared devices, such as a whiteboard or sticky notes.

Obviously, things have changed since, with life attitudes and work culture valuing home-working and flexibility more than stringent constraints on time and location. In addition, the recent COVID-19 pandemic acted as a catalyst for global adoption of remote working, and not only for software teams. Most organizations nowadays employ a remote workforce who work from different geographical locations, sometimes even in different time zones.

The question has now become *Can we still apply Scrum the way it was intended when our Scrum Team is fully remote?* The answer is yes, with a few adjustments. Let's take a look at the traditional Scrum tenets and practices that have been affected by the absence of co-location:

- **Communication**: The advantage of being co-located is that it's very easy to communicate. In most offices, asking the team a question meant simply shouting it out over your desk. As a Scrum Master or Product Owner, you could interact with organizational stakeholders or executives simply by locating them in the building. In remote teams, this is no longer the case.

- **Team rapport and morale**: The Scrum Team is meant to operate as a single, self-managed unit with a common goal. This is much easier when you know your teammates well and on a personal level. When all the teams are co-located, the daily trivial interactions between them build this rapport and help the team bond.

- **Collaboration**: When the whole team is in an office, they can gather around someone's computer in order to solve some coding problem. If they need to flesh out some new ideas, they will bring out the whiteboard and take turns on it. This is not as easy when working remotely.

- **Transparency**: People sometimes feel more isolated when working from home. As a result, they may feel more reluctant to share parts of their work, thoughts, or ideas.

It is primarily the Scrum Master's responsibility to suggest and implement methods to alleviate the preceding problems and foster a culture of openness, collaboration, and focus, as Scrum intended, even in remote teams (see *Chapter 2, Scrum Theory and Principles*). There are many ways to achieve this, dependent on the organization and the team's needs. Here are some suggestions:

- We can cultivate a culture of asynchronous communication. In the office, we are used to getting a response almost immediately after asking a question. This is not practical with remote teams, especially when people are working in different time zones. You can employ asynchronous communication by utilizing a messaging platform that supports different channels, which the team can organize by topic, product, or workstream.

  It may be a good idea to have a dedicated *urgent* channel, where people can post questions or issues that require urgent action or response. Team members can then set this channel up to send them immediate notifications to their cell phones. You'll need to ensure this channel doesn't get abused.

- We can replace synchronous Daily Scrums with online boards, where developers can describe their progress and any impediments, every day. Online forms may also serve the same function. Arrange a daily discussion about this board on a dedicated channel on your messaging app.

- We can create time and channels for personal interaction. For instance, you could have a book-club channel, where team members can post their thoughts on their favorite books. This could be followed by a dedicated discussion or presentation by video link, every week or two.

  Another popular common activity is quiz days. Set aside some time on a Friday afternoon to run a quiz for the team. Persuade the organization to provide some prizes for the winners. Quizzes are great fun and a morale booster.

- We can invest in and promote good visualization and diagramming software. When face-to-face discussion isn't easily available, we need to boost our documentation and visualization efforts. As the old adage goes *A picture is worth a thousand words*. When using diagrams, make sure you use a common notation, such as UML, to provide common semantics for the whole team. Another advantage of diagramming is that it's persistent. A design, for instance, can be better understood with a well-drawn diagram that people can look up as needed, than with a dozen conversations that may be easily forgotten.

- We can use a wiki. Wikis are a great enhancer of asynchronous communication. They are very useful for capturing small details that you may not have time or opportunity to present during a video-link meeting. They can also be used to capture team ideas and suggestions and foster offline discussion about them.

- We can ensure transparency by ensuring the product backlog, Scrum Board, wiki, documentation, and meeting appointments are easily accessible by all stakeholders. To that end, we should prefer tools that have good exporting functionality and anonymous read-only access by generated URLS. Many tools allow for user notifications that could, for instance, facilitate stakeholders to get updates when the Scrum Artifacts (*Chapter 5, Scrum Artifacts*) are updated.

Applying Scrum in remote teams is a tricky challenge that can be overcome by using the right tools, processes, and attitude. In this section, we say that by slightly changing our team culture to adopt more asynchronous ways of working and equipping them with the right tools, we can make remote working with Scrum just as productive as co-location.

Now it's time to get acquainted with another issue Scrum Masters face, regardless of remote or co-located teams.

Managing technical debt

Technical debt is a software development concept. It reflects the implied cost of additional rework caused by choosing a quick and restrictive solution instead of a more comprehensive but slower one.

Technical debt is generally an issue that transcends Scrum and applies to any type of software development process or methodology. However, it is particularly prominent in Scrum due to its application of short, focused development iterations.

How is technical debt created?

Let's consider a simple example: Bob, a developer, is working on a task that requires the storing of customer and product details in a database. Bob creates a single database table and inputs the data for both customers and products in it. This solution works and will continue to work for as long as the number of customers and products is small.

However, as this number increases with time, the maintenance of that table will become more difficult, data duplication will occur, and debugging, or expanding customer and product functionality will become much more costly. Bob has done enough to solve the problem at hand but has not anticipated the potential problems his solution has caused, which will need to be eventually addressed. Bob has created technical debt.

Technical debt can be unintentional, as in Bob's case, but it may also be caused intentionally. The team may decide that a more comprehensive solution may be too expensive or risky to implement at that point in time and accept a simpler but more limiting solution that will need to be re-implemented at some point in the future.

There is also a kind of passive technical debt that is usually created due to a lack of knowledge or experience of a specific problem domain. For example, the developers may discover a better technical approach for an item they delivered two Sprints earlier. Another way of creating passive technical debt is when the definition of Done is upgraded to include more numerous or stricter criteria. Often this introduces rework in former product increments.

How to pay back technical debt

Technical debt is not mentioned in the Scrum Guide and there is no generic solution or approach for dealing with it. In my experience, the following steps help tackle it:

- We can include code reviews as part of the definition of Done. Code reviews help identify technical debt, as well as code bugs and defects.

- When technical debt is discovered, add it as an item in the Product Backlog. Make sure you reference the original item in which the debt was created. The item will then have to be ordered and estimated in the backlog and will have to be dealt with during a Sprint.

- We can foster transparency about technical debt. We can encourage people to think about it and report it when they discover it.

- During the Sprint Review event, we can bring up any technical debt created during the Sprint. This will help inform the stakeholders about the state and potential fragility of the product.

- We can be adding a technical debt item to each Sprint Backlog. For example, let's suppose our team's velocity is 25 and our Sprint Backlog contains items worth 20 story points. This means we can add another item worth 5 story points to the Sprint Backlog (see *Chapter 6, Planning and Estimating with Scrum*). We could then choose a technical debt item worth 5 points to add to the Sprint Backlog. By applying this practice of adding a technical debt item to our Sprint Backlog at every Sprint, we are ensuring that debt is tackled regularly and doesn't become a burden or a risk to the product development.

There is no single solution for managing or avoiding technical debt. It's all about trade-offs. Technical perfection and futureproofing must be balanced against the business and customer needs. As with most trade-offs, meeting them down in the middle usually works best.

Managing technical debt is not part of Scrum but it's something a Scrum Master will encounter sooner or later, and they must be equipped to deal with it. There is one more topic that is not addressed in the Scrum Guide, but a skilled Scrum Master should be aware of. Let's discuss it in the next section.

Scaling Scrum

Scrum, as we've already discussed, is all about working in small, focused teams off a single Product Backlog. It's the most efficient and productive way of delivering software. Sometimes, however, the product that needs to be delivered is so large and complex that having one small team is not adequate.

This presents the following conundrum: Scrum prescribes a small team of up to eight developers, one Scrum Master, and one Product Owner. *How can we have dozens of developers working on the product, all using Scrum?* The solution to this is actually simple: we can partition the product work in separate but related workstreams, or product components, and create a Scrum Team to work on delivering each component. Each team will have its own product backlog and will work like any independent Scrum Team does. The teams will have to regularly coordinate to ensure they don't get in each other's way and that they all work towards the same goal.

This approach is called **Scrum of Scrums**. It's a scaled version of Scrum and is an efficient way of connecting multiple teams and helping them work in coordination towards a common goal. Each team works as they normally would within Scrum. However, the main difference is that each team appoints a delegate to regularly attend meetings with the delegates of all other teams. This Scrum of Scrums meeting is where cross-team coordination takes place, as depicted in the following diagram:

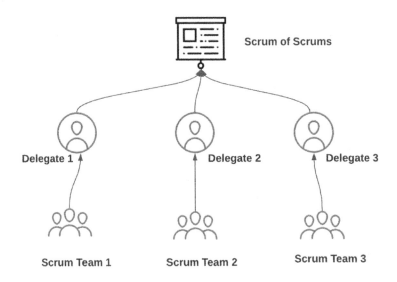

Figure 8.4 – Scrum of Scrums

The team delegate is normally the Scrum Master, but any team member with a good technical knowledge and product awareness could be the delegate. Unlike the daily Scrum meetings, the Scrum of Scrums meeting is not held every day. It depends on the number of teams involved, but this meeting usually happens one to three times a week.

The Scrum of Scrums meeting agenda is slightly different than the daily Scrum's agenda. Each delegate answers the following questions:

1. *What has my team done since the last meeting?*

2. *What is my team planning to do until the next meeting?*

3. *Does my team have any impediments?*

4. *Is any other team's work interfering or overlapping with my team's work?*

There is no prescribed time-box for the Scrum of Scrums meeting, but it's usually assigned a 30- to 60-minute duration.

The Scrum of Scrums is the simplest solution to scaling Scrum. You should bear in mind that there are also other scaling approaches and frameworks, such as **Large-scale Scrum (LeSS)** (`https://less.works`), **Nexus** (`https://www.scrum.org/resources/online-nexus-guide`), and **Scrum@Scale** (`https://www.scrumatscale.com`). However, they all introduce extra complexity, events, and artifacts to Scrum, so they should be applied only when absolutely necessary.

Summary

In this chapter, we examined topics that are outside the Scrum Guide but are very likely to be encountered in real life. A competent Scrum Master will be aware of these topics and will know what to do when confronted by them. We started by learning how a CI/CD pipeline enhances the development cadence and optimizes the value produced in the Sprint.

We also learned how to apply different testing levels to ensure a high level of quality and enhance our definition of Done. We talked about the things to do in order to foster the Scrum values when working remotely and how to tackle the issue of technical debt. Finally, we discussed how to apply Scrum when working with big teams and large products.

In the next chapter, we'll focus on the **Professional Scrum Master TM level I (PSM I)** assessment itself. You will learn how to prepare for the assessment and will test yourself against sample PSM I questions.

Questions

1. What does the practice of Continuous Integration involve? (Choose one answer.)

    a) Continuously merging code back into the main branch

    b) Continuously integrating external code into your local branch

    c) Continuously running tests on your code

    d) Continuously deploying code to users

2. Why are CI/CD pipelines important? (Choose three answers.)

    a) They implement a constant feedback loop by automatically exposing Product Increments to stakeholders.

    b) They leave developers free to concentrate on writing software instead of managing infrastructure.

    c) They eliminate all defects.

    d) They provide more frequent and earlier opportunities for defects to be exposed.

3. What determines when software should be deployed to a production environment, that is, released to users? (Choose all that apply.)

    a) The product owner's approval

    b) The result of automated tests

    c) Developers' approval

    d) The Definition of Done

4. What is technical debt? (Choose one answer.)

    a) The debt created when one developer helps another to complete a task

    b) The concept of using old or under-performing technologies for our development

    c) When developers decide to remove items from the Sprint Backlog

    d) The implied cost of additional rework caused by choosing a quick and restrictive solution instead of a more comprehensive but slower one

5. What is the Scrum of Scrums? (Choose three answers.)

    a) The event at the end of product development

    b) A way of scaling the Scrum

    c) A regular meeting of the delegates of different Scrum Teams to discuss their overall progress toward a common goal

    d) A method applied when a single Scrum Team is not enough to deliver a large and complex product

Section 3: The PSM Certification

In this part, you will learn how to prepare and practice for the PSM I exam.

This section comprises the following chapter:

- *Chapter 9, Preparing for the PSM I Assessment*

9
Preparing for the PSM I Assessment

In this chapter, we will focus on the **Professional Scrum Master I (PSM I)** assessment exam. We will ensure that you are prepared and ready to take the assessment, to maximize your chances of passing and becoming a PSM I Scrum Master. We'll discuss what you need to do before, during, and after the assessment. In detail, we will cover the following topics:

- Getting ready for the PSM I assessment
- Taking the PSM I assessment
- PSM I mock assessment

By the end of the chapter, you will feel confident and ready to start taking the next steps toward becoming a PSM I-certified Scrum Master.

Getting ready for the PSM I assessment

The PSM I assessment is an assessment offered by Scrum.org to certify a fundamental understanding of Scrum. The PSM I certificate is evidence of the holder's understanding of Scrum, as described in the *Scrum Guide*, and their ability to apply Scrum in Scrum Teams. There are no qualifications or preconditions needed to take the assessment. You don't need to take a Scrum.org course in order to take the assessment (though it would certainly help).

Scrum.org also offers two more Scrum Master assessments (PSM II and PSM III) that test more advanced Scrum knowledge. The assessment costs **US dollars (USD)** $150 and is taken online at `https://www.scrum.org/professional-scrum-certifications/professional-scrum-master-assessments`. You must be registered with Scrum.org to take the assessment. If you fail the assessment, you can retake it almost immediately. The $150 fee must, however, be paid every time you take the assessment.

Fundamental information about the assessment

The assessment consists of 80 questions, with a time limit of 60 minutes. The assessments are presented in the English language. Most questions use clear and uncomplicated English, so non-native speakers with a conversational grasp of English should not be at a big disadvantage. Some key points to know about the assessment are given here:

- The questions are all multiple-choice and come in varying formats:

  a) Questions where you choose one single correct answer.

  b) Questions where you choose multiple correct answers. The question will usually tell you how many correct answers there are.

  c) Questions with a binary answer, where you choose between True and False or Yes and No.

- The assessment questions cover the following four subject areas:

  a) Scrum theory and principles

  b) Scrum framework

  c) Coaching and facilitation

  d) Cross-functional and self-managing teams

- The pass mark is 85%. Not all questions are weighted equally, so do not assume you only need to correctly answer 68 (80 x 85%) questions to pass. The weights of the questions are not made known.

- The assessment provides the functionality to bookmark questions you cannot easily answer or are unsure of, so you can revisit them after the final question (assuming you have enough time).

What you will need to take the assessment

The assessment is taken online, so you don't need to visit a test facility. To take the assessment you will need a computer, a quiet room (this is for your own sake—the assessment does not require audio input), and a reasonably fast and reliable internet connection. It is also advisable to keep the following nearby: a drink, some tissues, a food snack, and anything else you may require during the following 60 minutes. This will ensure you won't have to leave the room and therefore break your concentration and disrupt your train of thought.

In the case of technical issues, such as the internet connection dropping, email `support@scrum.org` for further instructions. If possible, take a screenshot of the error message and attach it to your email.

How to prepare for the assessment

Here are some tips to prepare you for taking the assessment:

- The best thing you can do is learn as much about Scrum as you can. Apart from this book, it's a good idea to read books by Ken Schwaber and Jeff Sutherland, the Scrum founders. Particularly recommended are the following:

  a) *Software in 30 Days*, Wiley Publishing, 2012

  b) *Scrum: The Art of Doing Twice the Work in Half the Time*, Random House Business, 2015

- Study the resources available on Scrum.org (`https://www.scrum.org/pathway/scrum-master`). The sidebar lists all relevant areas—make sure you study everything under the *Understanding and Applying Scrum* topic.

- Something to consider when reading material on Scrum is the *Scrum Guide* revisions. The *Scrum Guide* is regularly updated, and the advice it provides is modified to reflect current thinking and latest practices. The latest *Scrum Guide* edition was published in November 2020 and it has some significant modifications over the previous 2017 edition. Make sure the material you are reading is compatible with the 2020 edition of the *Scrum Guide*. This book is fully updated with the latest 2020 guidelines.

- Exercise extreme caution when attending online preparatory courses for PSM I. In my experience, many of them give misleading and confusing advice, and even provide wrong answers in their quizzes. Make sure you are coached only by reputable publishers and authors.

- **Very important**: Take the Scrum Open assessment (`https://www.scrum.org/open-assessments/scrum-open`). This is a test assessment, put together by `Scrum.org`, and it is provided in the style and structure of the actual, real assessment. In fact, questions in the Open assessment often appear in the actual PSM I assessment itself. Do not attempt to take the PSM I assessment until you are scoring a minimum of 95% in the open assessment. Aim to be able to get to the last Open assessment question within 50 minutes. This will give you 10 minutes to revisit any bookmarked questions. Keep taking the Open assessment until you've reached the aforementioned levels of efficiency.

Now that you know how to prepare for the assessment, let's see what you need to do while taking the assessment.

Taking the PSM I assessment

So, you have booked your PSM I assessment. You're sitting in front of the computer, the assessment has been loaded, and you are about to click the **Start** button. You are confident in your abilities (because you have read this book) but want to make sure you don't fall at this last hurdle. Here's what you should be doing:

- Make sure you've booked the exam at the time of your maximum mental ability. For most people this is early morning, but different people may perform best at different times.

- Don't have a large meal or drink alcohol in the hours before the assessment. Both these things affect your ability to think clearly.

- Don't take longer than 40 seconds on any one question. If after that time period you're still not sure what the correct answer is, bookmark the question and move on to the next one. You'll be able to revisit bookmarked questions after the final one.

- Do not leave any questions unanswered. Even guessing the answer gives you some odds of being correct. Unanswered questions give you no chance of success.

- Do not be tempted to look up answers on the internet or in the *Scrum Guide*. The assessment is structured in such a way that wasting valuable time looking up answers is a sure way to fail.

- Do not leave your computer unless you really must. Not only are you going to waste precious time, but your train of thought will also be disrupted.

Being mentally and physically prepared and having a strategy during the assessment will maximize your chances of success.

What happens after the assessment

At the end of the assessment, you will be presented with your score as well as some general feedback on how you've performed in the assessment's subject areas (see the *Fundamental information about the assessment* section of this chapter). If you are successful, you will receive your certificate by email and your name will be added to Scrum.org's certification list (`https://www.scrum.org/certification-list`).

If you haven't passed, do not despair. Examine the feedback and identify the areas where you didn't do well. Study more on those areas, keep taking the Scrum Open assessment, and retake the PSM I when you're feeling more confident.

We're going to wrap up this chapter with a mock assessment questionnaire, giving you a chance to test your knowledge against all subject areas of the PSM I.

PSM I mock assessment

1. When might a Sprint be canceled? (choose the best answer)

    a) When the Developers feel they cannot complete the Sprint

    b) When the Sprint Goal becomes obsolete

    c) When senior management asks the team to work on something else

    d) When more than one Developer falls ill

2. When does the next Sprint begin? (choose the best answer)

    a) When the Product Owner gives the go-ahead

    b) Immediately following the next Sprint Planning

    c) On a Monday

    d) Immediately after the conclusion of the previous Sprint

3. Which is part of the Scrum Master's responsibilities regarding the Daily Scrum? (choose the best answer)

    a) Asking the Developers about their progress since the last Daily Scrum

    b) Making sure each Developer has a chance to speak

    c) Coaching the Developers to keep the Daily Scrum within a 15-minute time-box

    d) All answers apply

4. How is the Product Backlog ordered? (choose the best answer)

    a) In whichever way the Product Owner deems appropriate

    b) With the most valuable items at the top

    c) With the most complex items at the top

    d) With the riskiest items at the bottom

    e) In whichever way the Scrum Master deems appropriate

5. Who is responsible for managing the progress of work during a Sprint? (choose the best answer)

    a) The Scrum Master

    b) The Team Leader

    c) The Product Owner

    d) The Developers

6. The Developers should not be interrupted during the Sprint, and the Sprint Goal should remain intact. These are conditions that foster creativity, quality, and productivity. Which one of the following statements is false?

    a) The Sprint Backlog is fully formed in the Sprint Planning event and does not change during the Sprint.

    b) The Developers may add more work to the Sprint Backlog if this is needed in order to reach the Sprint Goal.

    c) The Developers may work with the Product Owner to remove or add work if they find it has more or less capacity than expected.

    d) The Product Owner can help clarify or optimize the Sprint Goal when asked by the Developers.

7. Which statement best describes a Product Owner's responsibility? (choose the best answer)

    a) Keeping stakeholders from distracting the Developers

    b) Ensuring the Developers deliver the agreed work

    c) Optimizing the value of the work the Scrum Team does

    d) Managing the Developers' productivity

8. What is the role of Management in Scrum? (choose the best answer)

    a) Supporting the Product Owner by providing information about product strategy and market conditions, and facilitating access to stakeholders. Supporting the Scrum Master, to promote understanding and adoption of Scrum within the organization.

    b) Replacing Developers who underperform.

    c) Monitoring the progress of the Scrum Team to ensure that deadlines are met.

    d) Ensuring the Scrum Team is keeping within its budget.

9. Who is on a Scrum Team? (choose the best three answers)

    a) Developers

    b) The Project Manager

    c) The Scrum Master

    d) The Product Owner

10. During a Sprint, a Developer determines that the Scrum Team will not be able to complete the items in their forecast. Who should be present to review and adjust the Product Backlog items selected? (choose the best three answers)

    a) The Product Owner and the Stakeholders

    b) The Product Owner and the Developers

    c) The Product Owner and the Scrum Master

    d) The Developers only

11. When does a Developer become accountable for the value of a Product Backlog item selected for a Sprint? (choose the best answer)

    a) At the Sprint Planning Event

    b) During the Daily Scrum

    c) Whenever they are assigned a backlog item

    d) Never—the entire Scrum Team is accountable for creating value at every Sprint

12. Who creates the **Definition of Done (DoD)**? (choose the best answer)

    a) If it is not already an organizational standard, the Scrum Team must create an appropriate DoD for the product.

    b) The Scrum Master, with the help of the Developers.

    c) The Scrum Master alone.

    d) The Product Owner.

13. Who has the final say on the order of the Product Backlog? (choose the best answer)

    a) The Stakeholders

    b) The Project Manager

    c) The Developers

    d) The Product Owner

    e) The Scrum Master

14. The Developers should have all the skills needed to (choose the best answer):

    a) Do all the development work except for testing, which should be done by the testing team.

    b) Turn the Product Backlog items they select into an Increment of useful and valuable product functionality.

    c) Turn the Product Backlog items the Scrum Master selects into an Increment of useful and valuable product functionality.

    d) Implement the tasks given to them by the Product Owner.

15. It is mandatory that the Product Increment be released to production at the end of each Sprint. True or false?

    a) True

    b) False

16. Why is the Daily Scrum held at the same time and the same place? (choose the best answer)

    a) It promotes consistency and reduces complexity.

    b) So that the Product Owner can monitor the Developers more easily.

    c) So that Management knows where and when to get updates.

17. What is the time-box for a Daily Scrum? (choose the best answer)

    a) 2 minutes per Developer.

    b) 30 minutes.

    c) 15 minutes.

    d) 15 minutes for a 4-week sprint. For shorter Sprints, it is usually shorter.

18. Which Scrum Events are time-boxed? (choose the best three answers)

    a) Sprint Review

    b) Product Backlog refinement

    c) Release planning

    d) Product Roadmap Review

    e) Sprint Planning

    f) Sprint Retrospective

19. Which of the following are examples of a Scrum Team practicing Scrum poorly or not exhibiting the traits of a self-managing Scrum Team? (choose the best three answers)

    a) The Developers are collaboratively selecting their own work during the Sprint.

    b) The Developers create their own Sprint Backlog, reflecting all work that is required to meet the DoD.

    c) Stakeholders attend the Daily Scrum to check on the Scrum Team's progress.

    d) The Developers have all the skills they need to create a valuable, useful Increment.

    e) The Developers invite external stakeholders to the Sprint Planning to help them estimate and order Product Backlog items.

    f) The Developers release an Increment to the testing team for verification.

20. What is the recommended size for a Scrum Team? (choose the best answer)

    a) 9

    b) 10 or fewer people

    c) 7—plus or minus 2

    d) No more than 7

21. When many Scrum Teams are working on a single product, which of the following sentences best describes the DoD? (choose the best answer)

    a) All Scrum Teams must have a DoD that makes their combined Increment valuable and useful.

    b) Each Scrum Team has its own, independent DoD.

    c) Scrum Teams that work on similar product features must have the same DoD.

22. When multiple Scrum Teams work together on the same product, each team should maintain a separate Product Backlog. True or false?

    a) True

    b) False

23. Which two things should the Developers do during the first Sprint? (choose the best two answers)

    a) Make up a plan for the rest of the project.

    b) Analyze, describe, and document the requirements for subsequent Sprints.

    c) Analyze, design, and describe the product's architecture and infrastructure.

    d) Create an Increment of potentially releasable software.

    e) Develop at least one piece of functionality.

24. The length of a Sprint should be (choose the best answer):

    a) 1 month or less

    b) Short enough to keep the business risk acceptable to the Product Owner

    c) Short enough to be able to synchronize development work with other business events

    d) All of the above

25. During the Daily Scrum, a Developer says they don't know when their task will be done. What is the correct action to take? (choose the best answer)

a) The Scrum Master mentors the Developer on how to estimate better.

b) The Developers decide to pair up on that task, in order to complete it by the end of the Sprint.

c) The Developers decide to replace the Developer with a new one.

d) Do nothing—uncertainty is part of software development.

Mock assessment answers

1. Question 1—correct answer: b

    A Sprint could be canceled if the Sprint Goal becomes obsolete. Only the Product Owner has the authority to cancel a Sprint.

2. Question 2—correct answer: d

    A new Sprint starts immediately after the conclusion of the previous Sprint.

3. Question 3—correct answer: c

    The Developers are responsible for conducting the Daily Scrum. The Scrum Master coaches the Developers to keep the Daily Scrum within the 15-minute time-box and ensures that only Developers participate in the Daily Scrum.

4. Question 4—correct answer: a

    The Product Owner is accountable for Product Backlog management. The Product Backlog is an emergent, ordered list of what is needed to improve a product. The order of the backlog is determined by the Product Owner and may be done based on business value, priority risk, or any other method the Product Owner deems appropriate. The Scrum Master may advise the Product Owner on ways of ordering the Product Backlog.

5. Question 5—correct answer: d

    The Developers use the Daily Scrum to inspect progress toward the Sprint Goal and monitor remaining work in the Sprint Backlog. There is no Team Leader role in a Scrum Team.

6. Question 6—correct answer: a

    The Sprint Backlog comprises all the work the Developers identify as necessary to meet the Sprint Goal. The Developers modify the Sprint Backlog throughout the Sprint as deemed necessary to achieve the Sprint Goal, and the Sprint Backlog emerges during the Sprint.

7. Question 7—correct answer: c

    The Product Owner is accountable for maximizing the value of the product and the work of the Scrum Team.

8. Question 8—correct answer: a

    Management has no active role in the actual product development through Scrum. However, they should act as enablers and guides for the overall direction of the organization.

9. Question 9—correct answer: a, c, d

    A Scrum Team consists of a Scrum Master, a Product Owner, and Developers.

10. Question 10—correct answer: b

    During a Sprint, the scope may be clarified and renegotiated between the Product Owner and the Developers as more is learned. It is important to be transparent when challenges arise since ultimately, the entire Scrum Team is accountable for creating a valuable, useful Increment.

11. Question 11—correct answer: d

    All members of the Scrum Team share accountability for creating value for every Sprint.

12. Question 12—correct answer: a

    If the DoD has already been defined by the organization, all Scrum Teams must follow it and build on it, if required. If it is not an organizational standard, the Scrum Team must create a DoD suitable for the product.

13. Question 13—correct answer: d

    The Product Owner is the sole person responsible for ordering the Product Backlog.

14. Question 14—correct answer: b

    The Developers are responsible for delivering an Increment of the done product at the end of the Sprint. As a team, Developers have all the skills necessary to create a Product Increment.

15. Question 15—correct answer: b

The Product Increment should be usable and releasable at the end of every Sprint, but it does not have to be released. The Product Owner will decide whether to release an Increment.

16. Question 16—correct answer: a

The Daily Scrum is held at the same time and place each day to foster consistency and reduce complexity.

17. Question 17—correct answer: c

The Daily Scrum is a 15-minute event, regardless of the team size or Sprint length.

18. Question 18—correct answer: a, e, f

The Sprint Planning, Sprint Retrospective, and Sprint Review are time-boxed events.

19. Question 19—correct answer: c, e, f

External stakeholders must not attend the Daily Scrum to check the progress of the Developers. During Sprint Planning, the Developers add items to the Sprint Backlog in order to meet the Sprint Goal. In Scrum, there is no separate testing team. Developers are responsible for ensuring their work meets the DoD.

20. Question 20—correct answer: b

A Scrum Team is small enough to remain flexible and large enough to complete significant work within a Sprint—typically, with 10 or fewer people.

21. Question 21—correct answer: a

When many Scrum Teams are working on a single product, they are expected to adhere to a single DoD for the Increment so that the Increment is valuable and useful.

22. Question 22—correct answer: b

There is only one Product Backlog per product, regardless of how many Scrum Teams are working on the product. This ensures that work is easily shared and not duplicated.

23. Question 23—correct answer: d, e

    A Sprint aims to create an Increment of potentially releasable software. This usually involves developing at least one piece of functionality. Design and infrastructure tasks may occur as part of any Sprint. Requirement analysis occurs during the Sprint Planning event. There is nothing special about the first, or any other, Sprint.

24. Question 24—correct answer: d

    The Sprint length should be short enough to maximize value, minimize risk, and keep work in sync with business events. The Sprint length should not exceed 1 month.

25. Question 25—correct answer: b

    The Developers must be focused on meeting the Sprint Goal, so ignoring the issue is not an option. If there is an impediment preventing a Developer from completing a task, it should be brought to the Scrum Master for resolution and can be discussed during the Sprint Retrospective for further action.

Summary

In this chapter, we focused on what to do to pass the PSM I assessment. We looked at several intellectual and physical steps we can take to maximize our chances of passing.

We discussed the importance of accessing the right material and updating to the latest guidelines. We emphasized the role of the Scrum Open assessment in our preparation and came up with a strategy for using the open assessment as our preparedness litmus test. We also examined what to do after the assessment, especially in the case of failure.

Finally, we wrapped up the knowledge gained in this book with a mock PSM I assessment questionnaire. At this point, you should have the required skills to take and pass the PSM I assessment. Thank you for reading this book, and I am confident you'll be joining the PSM club soon!

Assessments

This section contains answers to the questions posed in all chapters.

Chapter 2 – Scrum Theory and Principles

Answers

1. The correct answer is c.

   Scrum is a process framework, not a methodology or process.

2. The correct answer is c.

   Empiricism, the principle that underpins Scrum, is based on constant inspection and adaptation.

3. The correct answer is d.

   Openness means that we share both good and bad things with our team. By failing to mention the weaknesses of his design, Bob hasn't been open with the team.

4. The correct answer is b.

   Alice has been open to discussing alternative algorithms to the one she chose. She also showed courage in accepting a new algorithm, as suggested by the team, and implementing it.

5. The correct answer is d.

   By accepting to work on a non-Sprint item, Carol lost focus of the task she was working on and of the Sprint goal.

Chapter 3 – The Scrum Team

Answers

1. The correct answer is d.

    The Developers are self-managing and they are solely responsible for deciding how to deliver a Product Increment and which working practices to employ. Neither the Scrum Master, nor the Product Owner may interfere with the Developers' work.

2. The correct answer is b.

    Answer (d) is wrong, as the Developers estimate and select work items at the start of the Sprint and then commit to completing them.

    (a) and (c) are also wrong as the Scrum Master cannot interfere with the Developers' working practices.

    The Scrum Master may, however, guide them towards customizing or improving the Scrum process and suggesting a Sprint length increase (b) provides such guidance.

3. The correct answer is b.

    Answer (a) is clearly wrong, and (d) is the responsibility of the Scrum Master. The Product Owner does not manage the project, or the work being done, they are responsible for the product (c).

4. The correct answer is a.

    Although the Developers and Scrum Master may make suggestions about the ordering of the Product Backlog items, the final say always rests with the Product Owner. The stakeholders do not directly participate in the ordering of the backlog.

5. The correct answer is d.

    Being unsure about how a feature works is not an impediment, unless clarification cannot be gained (a). Clarity about the work being done is always needed and the person responsible to provide this is the Product Owner (d), not other team members (c).

6. The correct answer is c.

    Changes in the Developer group structure are disruptive and should be avoided. If a change must be made, a short-term disruption is to be expected.

7. The correct answer is d.

    The Developers are self-managing, solely responsible for their work during the Sprint.

Chapter 4 – Scrum Events

Answers

1. The correct answer is c.

    The Sprint Backlog should contain enough items to get the Sprint started but items may be added or removed during the Sprint by the Development Team.

2. The correct answer is a.

    Time-boxed events are events that have a maximum duration.

3. The correct answer is c.

    Sprint Planning is time-boxed to a maximum of 8 hours for a 1-month Sprint. For shorter Sprints, the event is usually shorter.

4. The correct answer is c.

    The Daily Scrum serves to inspect work done since the last Daily Scrum and plan work to be done in the next 24 hours.

5. The correct answer is e.

    The Sprint Planning duration is 4 hours for a monthly Sprint. For shorter Sprints, it is usually shorter.

6. The correct answer is b.

    To ensure continuous improvement, the Sprint Backlog should include at least one high-priority process improvement identified in the previous Sprint. The Product Backlog should only contain product-specific items.

7. The correct answer is b.

    The Definition of Done should change when it does not reflect the quality standards expected by the team, organization, or stakeholders. The decision to change it usually takes place during the Sprint Retrospective.

Chapter 5 – Scrum Artifacts

Answers

1. The correct answer is d.

   The items that have been selected for a Sprint have been selected as the most valuable to the Product Owner. The items serve the Sprint's goal. No changes should be made that endanger the Sprint Goal. No one external to the Scrum Team can force changes on the developers (Sprint Backlog) and the Product Owner (Product Backlog).

2. The correct answer is b.

   Products have one Product Backlog, regardless of how many teams are used. Any other setup makes it difficult for the developers to determine what to work on.

3. The correct answer is b.

   The Sprint Goal sets the direction and objectives for the Sprint.

4. The correct answer is a.

   Multiple Increments may be created within a Sprint. The sum of the Increments is presented at the Sprint Review, thus supporting empiricism. However, an Increment may be delivered to stakeholders prior to the end of the Sprint. The Sprint Review should never be considered a gate to releasing value.

5. The correct answer is d.

   The developers collectively own all the items in the Sprint Backlog.

6. The correct answer is a.

7. The correct answer is b.

   As per the Scrum Guide 2020, the Scrum Team creates the Definition of Done, unless an organization-wide definition already exists.

8. The correct answer is c.

   As per the Scrum Guide 2020, a Sprint is not confined to the release of a single increment at the end of the Sprint or Sprint Review. Many increments may be created during a Sprint and released as needed.

9. The correct answer is a.

   Refinement is an ongoing activity that should take place at regular intervals during the Sprint.

Chapter 6 – Planning and Estimating with Scrum

Answers

1. The correct answer is c.

    Story points are used to indicate relative size and complexity. They do not denote time units. It is impossible to know whether an item is feasible to be completed within a Sprint, based on its story points, unless we know the estimation scale and baseline.

2. The correct answers are a, c, and d.

    Having fixed dates in the product roadmap goes against Agile and Scrum principles of constant inspection and adaptation versus following a set plan.

3. The correct answer is c.

    Estimating methods such as planning poker rely on developers reaching consensus by providing individual estimates and then discussing the motivations behind the estimates until agreement is reached on a single estimate value.

4. The correct answer is c.

    Velocity is subjective to a specific team and product. It is not a comparative measurement.

5. The correct answer is b.

    Burn-up charts let us visualize progress over time. Roadmaps help to identify long-term goals and milestones. Velocity is used for charting and forecasting in the context of burn-up/down charts. Burn-down charts help to visualize work done as well as work remaining within a Sprint.

Chapter 7 – The Sprint Journey

Answers

1. The correct answers are a, b, and c.

    Creating tasks for delivering backlog items occurs after the items have been selected for the Sprint Backlog.

2. The correct answer is d.

    The product owner decides how the Product Backlog items are ordered. This can be by value, cost, risk, or other ways.

3. The correct answer is b.

    A Sprint should aim to create a valuable, working Product Increment. No Sprint is special.

4. The correct answer is c.

    The only reason to cancel the Sprint is when the Sprint goal becomes redundant. This should be a very rare occasion.

5. The correct answer is a.

    If a defect is discovered on an item currently worked on, this usually indicates some unanticipated condition and unforeseen extra work. In the interests of transparency, this should be captured on a board card and placed in the Sprint Backlog. It will be picked up and worked on as the Sprint progresses. There is no need to interfere with the Product Backlog or disrupt the Sprint.

Chapter 8 – Facets of Scrum

Answers

1. The correct answer is a.

    The practice of **Continuous Integration** (**CI**) involves continuously merging code back into the main branch.

2. The correct answers are a, b, and d.

    CI/CD pipelines do not eliminate defects; however, they do provide more frequent and earlier opportunities for defects to be exposed. They also enable constant feedback, which comes from constantly releasing increments to stakeholders.

3. The correct answers are a and b.

    The Definition of Done determines when a backlog item has been completed, not when software can be released. This is up to the product owner and the testing setup on the CI/CD pipeline.

4. The correct answer is d.

    Technical debt is the implied cost of additional rework caused by choosing a quick and restrictive solution instead of a more comprehensive but slower one.

5. The correct answers are b, c, and d.

    The Scrum of Scrums is a method for scaling Scrum, usually applied when the product is too large and complex for a single Scrum Team. The term is derived from the name of the regular meeting between the delegates of the various Scrum Teams.

Packt.com

Subscribe to our online digital library for full access to over 7,000 books and videos, as well as industry leading tools to help you plan your personal development and advance your career. For more information, please visit our website.

Why subscribe?

- Spend less time learning and more time coding with practical eBooks and Videos from over 4,000 industry professionals

- Improve your learning with Skill Plans built especially for you

- Get a free eBook or video every month

- Fully searchable for easy access to vital information

- Copy and paste, print, and bookmark content

Did you know that Packt offers eBook versions of every book published, with PDF and ePub files available? You can upgrade to the eBook version at packt.com and as a print book customer, you are entitled to a discount on the eBook copy. Get in touch with us at customercare@packtpub.com for more details.

At www.packt.com, you can also read a collection of free technical articles, sign up for a range of free newsletters, and receive exclusive discounts and offers on Packt books and eBooks.

Other Books You May Enjoy

If you enjoyed this book, you may be interested in these other books by Packt:

Scaling Scrum Across Modern Enterprises

Cecil Rupp

ISBN: 978-1-83921-647-3

- Understand the limitations of traditional Scrum practices
- Explore the roles and responsibilities in a scaled Scrum and Lean-Agile development environment
- Tailor your Scrum approach to support portfolio and large product development needs
- Apply systems thinking to evaluate the impacts of changes in the interdependent parts of a larger development and delivery system
- Scale Scrum practices at both the program and portfolio levels of management
- Understand how DevOps, test automation, and CI/CD capabilities help in scaling Scrum practices

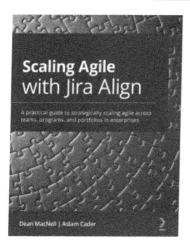

Scaling Agile with Jira Align

Dean MacNeil , Aslam Cader

ISBN: 978-1-80020-321-1

- Understand Jira Align's key factors for success
- Find out how you can connect people, work, time, and outcomes with Jira Align
- Navigate and collaborate in Jira Align
- Scale team agility to the portfolio and enterprise
- Delve into planning and execution, including roadmaps and predictability metrics
- Implement lean portfolio management and OKRs
- Get to grips with handling bimodal and hybrid delivery
- Enable advanced data security and analytics in Jira Align

Packt is searching for authors like you

If you're interested in becoming an author for Packt, please visit `authors.packtpub.com` and apply today. We have worked with thousands of developers and tech professionals, just like you, to help them share their insight with the global tech community. You can make a general application, apply for a specific hot topic that we are recruiting an author for, or submit your own idea.

Share Your Thoughts

Now you've finished *The Professional Scrum Master (PSM I) Guide*, we'd love to hear your thoughts! Scan the QR code below to go straight to the Amazon review page for this book and share your feedback.

`https://packt.link/r/1800205562`

Your review is important to us and the tech community and will help us make sure we're delivering excellent quality content.

Index

Made in the USA
Columbia, SC
02 January 2023

75388198R00096